STECK-VAUGHN

W9-BDS-786

WORKING *with* **Numbers**

LEVEL F

Acknowledgments
Cover Photo: © Chris Tomaidis /Stone

ISBN 0-7398-9161-8

ISBN 978-0-7398-9161-2

Harcourt Achieve
Rigby · Steck-Vaughn

www.HarcourtAchieve.com
1.800.531.5015

Table of Contents

LEVEL F

Unit 1 Whole Numbers and Operations

Place Value 4
Comparing and Ordering 5
Addition of Whole Numbers 6
Addition of 3 or More Numbers 7
Subtraction of Whole Numbers 8–9
Estimation of Sums 10
Estimation of Differences 11
Problem-Solving Strategy:
    Guess & Check 12–13
Problem-Solving Applications 14
Multiplication of 1-digit Numbers 15
Zeros in Multiplication 16
Multiplication of 2-digit Numbers 17
Multiplication of 3-digit Numbers 18
Estimation of Products 19
1-digit Divisors with Remainders 20
Dividing by Multiples of 10 21
Trial Quotient: Too Large or Too Small . .22
Zeros in Quotients 23
2-digit Divisors with Remainders 24
Estimation of Quotients 25
Problem-Solving Strategy:
    Choose an Operation 26–27
Problem-Solving Applications 28
Unit 1 Review 29–31

Unit 2 Fractions

Meaning of Fractions 32
Improper Fractions and
    Mixed Numbers 33
Equivalent Fractions 34
Simplifying Fractions 35
Addition and Subtraction of Fractions
    with Like Denominators 36
Addition of Fractions with Different
    Denominators 37
Addition of Fractions Using the
    Least Common Denominator 38–39

Problem-Solving Strategy:
    Make a Graph 40–41
Problem-Solving Applications 42
Adding Mixed Numbers, Whole
    Numbers, and Fractions 43
Adding Mixed Numbers with
    Large Sums 44–45
Subtraction of Fractions with Different
    Denominators 46–47
Subtraction of Fractions and Mixed
    Numbers from Whole Numbers . . .48–49
Subtraction of Mixed Numbers
    with Regrouping 50–51
Problem-Solving Strategy:
    Use Estimation 52–53
Problem-Solving Applications 54
Unit 2 Review 55–57

Unit 3 Multiplication and Division of Fractions

Multiplication of Fractions 58
Multiplication of Fractions Using
    Cancellation 59
Multiplication of Whole Numbers
    by Fractions 60–61
Multiplication of Mixed Numbers
    by Whole Numbers 62
Multiplication of Mixed Numbers
    by Fractions 63
Multiplication of Mixed Numbers
    by Mixed Numbers 64–65
Problem-Solving Strategy:
    Solve Multi-Step Problems 66–67
Problem-Solving Applications 68
Finding Reciprocals 69
Division of Fractions by Fractions . . .70–71
Division of Fractions by Whole
    Numbers 72–73
Division of Whole Numbers by
    Fractions 74
Division of Mixed Numbers by
    Whole Numbers 75
Division of Mixed Numbers by
    Fractions 76

Division of Mixed Numbers by
Mixed Numbers **77**
Problem-Solving Strategy:
Write a Number Sentence **78–79**
Problem-Solving Applications **80**
Unit 3 Review **81–83**

Unit 4 Decimals

Reading and Writing Decimals **84**
Comparing and Ordering Decimals **85**
Fraction and Decimal Equivalents . . .**86–87**
Problem-Solving Strategy:
Use Logic **88–89**
Problem-Solving Applications **90**
Rounding Decimals **91**
Addition and Subtraction of
Decimals **92–93**
Estimation of Decimal Sums and
Differences **94–95**
Problem-Solving Strategy:
Work Backwards **96–97**
Problem-Solving Applications **98**
Unit 4 Review **99–101**

Unit 5 Multiplication and Division of Decimals

Multiplying by Powers of Ten **102**
Multiplying Decimals by Whole
Numbers **103**
Multiplying Decimals by
Decimals **104–105**
Problem-Solving Strategy:
Identify Extra Information **106–107**
Problem-Solving Applications **108**
Dividing by Powers of Ten **109**
Dividing Decimals by Whole
Numbers **110–111**
Dividing Decimals by Decimals . . .**112–113**
Dividing Whole Numbers by
Decimals **114–115**
Decimal Quotients **116**

Rounding Quotients **117**
Problem-Solving Strategy:
Complete a Pattern **118–119**
Problem-Solving Applications **120**
Unit 5 Review **121–123**

Unit 6 Measurement

Customary Length **124**
Customary Weight **125**
Customary Capacity **126**
Computing Measures **127**
Metric Length **128**
Metric Mass **129**
Metric Capacity **130**
Computing Metric Measures **131**
Problem-Solving Strategy:
Make an Organized List **132–133**
Problem-Solving Applications **134**
Unit 6 Review **135–137**

Unit 7 Geometry

Points, Lines, and Planes **138–139**
Angles **140–141**
Congruent Segments
and Angles **142–143**
Problem-Solving Strategy:
Make a Drawing **144–145**
Perimeter of a Rectangle **146**
Formula for Perimeter of a
Rectangle **147**
Area of a Rectangle **148**
Formula for Area of a Rectangle **149**
Volume of a Rectangular Solid **150**
Formula for Volume of a
Rectangular Solid **151**
Problem-Solving Strategy:
Use a Formula **152–153**
Problem-Solving Applications **154**
Unit 7 Review **155–156**

Final Review **157–160**

Place Value

A **place-value chart** can help you understand **whole numbers.** Each **digit** in a number has a value based on its place in the number.

The digit 6 means 6 ten thousands, or 60,000.
The digit 2 means 2 thousands, or 2,000.
The digit 0 means 0 hundreds, or 0.
The digit 4 means 4 tens, or 40.
The digit 0 means 0 ones, or 0.

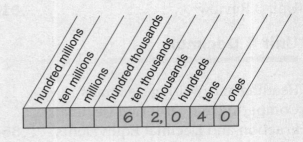

We read the number as sixty-two thousand, forty. Notice that commas are used to separate the digits into groups of three, called **periods.** This helps make larger numbers easier to read.

PRACTICE

Write each number in the place-value chart.

1. 468,937,574

2. 5,910,382,654

3. 8,342,384

4. 76,098

billions	hundred millions	ten millions	millions	hundred thousands	ten thousands	thousands	hundreds	tens	ones
1.	4	6	8,	9	3	7,	5	7	4
2.									
3.									
4.									

Write the place name for the digit 3 in each number.

	a		*b*
5. 56,837,784	ten thousands	887,654,321	
6. 90,543		675,345,242	
7. 898,865,436		3,876,544,098	
8. 3,565		24,356,540,912	

Write each number in words. Insert commas where needed.

9. 132,342   one hundred thirty-two thousand, three hundred forty-two

10. 7,642,353

Comparing and Ordering

To compare two numbers, begin with the highest place value.
Compare the digits in each place.

The symbol < means **is less than.**   *23 < 57*

The symbol > means **is greater than.**   *3 > 1*

The symbol = means **is equal to.**   *234 = 234*

Compare 354 and 57.

3	5	4	3 > 0, so
0	5	7	354 > 57.

Compare 2,243 and 1,542.

2,	2	4	3	2 > 1, so
1,	5	4	2	2,243 > 1,542.

Compare 134 and 187.

1	3	4	The hundreds digits are the same. Compare the tens digits.
1	8	7	

3 < 8, so 134 < 187.

PRACTICE

Compare. Write <, >, or =.

	a	b	c
1.	45 __<__ 67	165 _____ 85	33 _____ 36
2.	23 _____ 57	34 _____ 598	76 _____ 87
3.	675 _____ 765	654 _____ 654	764 _____ 761
4.	4,554 _____ 6,368	4,342 _____ 4,367	4,632 _____ 8,574
5.	653 _____ 785	4,321 _____ 824	3,242 _____ 6,543
6.	65,342 _____ 85,542	4,575 _____ 39,864	75,323 _____ 97,443
7.	973,765 _____ 1,000,000	453,643 _____ 255,764	3,400 _____ 3,399

Write in order from least to greatest.

8. 54   96   21 _____   *21   54   96*

9. 468   532   487 _____

10. 322   231   632 _____

11. 94,234   45,875   67,956 _____

12. 87,654   26,432   542,976 _____

13. 347,987   254,975   54,885 _____

14. 765,645   543,865   565,978 _____

15. 432,754   54,734   496,753 _____

16. 16,576   13,764   432,877 _____

Addition of Whole Numbers

To add, start with the digits in the ones place.
Regroup as needed.

Find: 322 + 699

	Add the ones. Regroup.	Add the tens.	Add the hundreds.

	Th	H	T	O
			1	
		3	2	2
+		6	9	9
				1

	Th	H	T	O
			1	1
		3	2	2
+		6	9	9
			2	1

	Th	H	T	O
		1	1	1
		3	2	2
+		6	9	9
	1,	0	2	1

PRACTICE

Add.

	a	b	c	d

1.

a:
```
 Th H T O
    1 1 1
    4 5 2
 +  5 5 9
 1, 0 1 1
```
b:
```
 Th H T O
    6 4 4
 +  4 8 4
```
c:
```
 Th H T O
    5 1 7
 +  5 6 3
```
d:
```
 Th H T O
    2 0 9
 +  9 5 0
```

2.

a:
```
  9 5 8
+ 5 3 2
```
b:
```
  3 2 1
+ 6 9 7
```
c:
```
 8,0 3 1
+4,8 6 5
```
d:
```
 5,4 5 3
+2,1 0 8
```

3.

a:
```
 5,3 4 7
+9,5 2 0
```
b:
```
 1 5,0 4 2
+8 6,9 9 6
```
c:
```
 3 4,8 5 3
+4 7,5 3 2
```
d:
```
 5 4 7,0 8 4
+7 4 3,7 5 4
```

4.

a:
```
 3 4 2,5 3 5
+7 5 7,6 4 3
```
b:
```
 7 4,5 7 4
+9 3,7 4 3
```
c:
```
 3 5 5,6 8 4
+8 9 5,4 4 5
```
d:
```
 5 4 6,7 8 3
+3 5 6,5 3 7
```

Line up the digits. Then find the sums.

	a	b	c

5. 6,535 + 5,764 = _____   543 + 528 = _____   532,743 + 23,907 = _____

```
 6,535
+5,764
```

6. 231,456 + 76,421 = _____   341 + 4,352 = _____   6,542 + 42,348 = _____

Addition of 3 or More Numbers

To add 3 or more numbers, use the same steps as when adding two numbers. Regroup as needed.

Find: 36 + 358 + 296

Add the ones. Regroup.	Add the tens.	Add the hundreds.
H T O 　2 　3 6 3 5 8 +2 9 6 　　 0	H T O 1 2 　3 6 3 5 8 +2 9 6 　9 0	H T O 1 2 　3 6 3 5 8 +2 9 6 6 9 0

PRACTICE

Add.

	a	b	c	d
1.	Th H T O 1 1 1 　4 2 7 　　7 8 +　8 4 3 1, 3 4 8	Th H T O 　　2 0 　6 5 9 + 9 3 2	Th H T O 　　　7 　6 4 3 +　6 7	Th H T O 　3 2 5 　8 9 6 +　　4
2.	3 9 3 4 2 +6 9 0	4 7 9 7 5 6 + 5 7	8 7 9 3,9 5 0 +　 4 3	3,4 0 4 8 6 5 +7,4 3 6
3.	9 3 9,8 4 2 8 7 4,8 9 0 　4 5,3 7 6 +4 3 2,9 8 6	6 3,9 2 8 3 2,7 4 0 　5,3 2 1 +6 0,4 5 3	8 4 9,9 0 4 4 3 2,8 4 0 5 0 8,3 4 6 +5 6 7,7 8 5	5 8 9,4 9 3 7 4 3,9 0 7 9 0 8,3 5 4 +5 6 7,8 6 9

Line up the digits. Then find the sums.

a

4. 554 + 860 + 64 = _____

554
860
+ 64

b

379 + 940 + 390 = _____

Subtraction of Whole Numbers

To subtract, start with the digits in the ones place.
Regroup as needed.

Find: 715 − 239

Regroup. Subtract the ones.	Regroup. Subtract the tens.	Subtract the hundreds.
H T O	H T O	H T O
0 15	6 10 15	6 10 15
7 1̶ 5̶	7̶ 1̶ 5̶	7̶ 1̶ 5̶
− 2 3 9	− 2 3 9	− 2 3 9
6	7 6	4 7 6

GUIDED PRACTICE

Subtract.

	a	b	c	d
1.	H T O 11 7 1̶ 17 8̶ 2 7 − 5 3 8 2 8 9	H T O 7 4 2 − 5 4 4	H T O 1 3 5 − 1 2 9	H T O 6 5 6 − 5 0 7
2.	H T O 9 3 10 10 4̶ 0̶ 0̶ − 1 2 5 2 7 5	H T O 7 0 0 − 4 0 4	H T O 8 0 0 − 4 5 1	H T O 5 0 0 − 4 3 0
3.	H T O 4 2 6 − 3 7	H T O 8 5 0 − 9 6	H T O 5 0 7 − 8 5	H T O 9 6 2 − 9 2
4.	Th H T O 6, 0 3 5 − 3, 9 7 4	Th H T O 2, 3 1 0 − 7 5 9	Th H T O 6, 3 6 4 − 4, 1 5 9	Th H T O 7, 0 9 5 − 3, 6 9 6

PRACTICE

Subtract.

	a	*b*	*c*	*d*
1.	8 9 4 −5 3 4	7 5 4 −4 4 5	8 6 4 − 4 9	9 0 7 −4 5 3
2.	5 4 3 −1 8 9	7 0 0 −5 4 6	5,0 0 0 − 8 9 9	7,6 4 3 −4,9 0 8
3.	5,7 6 4 − 2 0 0	4 3,6 7 5 −2 3,5 0 7	1 3,3 8 7 − 7,5 7 3	5 4,9 7 4 −3 4,5 5 6
4.	6 5 4,1 9 8 −4 6 5,3 9 7	7 8 1,0 3 5 − 3 5,4 6 7	4 3 9,7 0 9 −2 3 4,5 6 4	7 4 2,4 5 7 − 6 5,3 4 5

Line up the digits. Then find the differences.

a	*b*	*c*
5. 543 − 32 = _____	726 − 549 = _____	45,578 − 676 = _____

   543
− 32

a	*b*	*c*
6. 34,565 − 23,597 = _____	9,000 − 6,533 = _____	543,434 − 290,563 = _____

MIXED PRACTICE

Write in order from least to greatest.

a	*b*
1. 35 92 29 _____	63 38 90 _____
2. 8,900 679 2,809 _____	756 573 872 _____

Line up the digits. Then add.

a	*b*	*c*
3. 544 + 324 = _____	79 + 764 = _____	34,785 + 45,894 = _____

Estimation of Sums

To estimate a sum, first round each number to the same place.
Then add the rounded numbers.

Estimate: 56,493 + 255

Round each number to the same place. Add.

$$
\begin{array}{r}
5\,6{,}4\,9\,3 \to 56{,}500 \\
+\quad 2\,5\,5 \to +\quad 300 \\
\hline
56{,}800
\end{array}
$$

Each number is rounded to the hundreds place.

Estimate: 3,680 + 2,320

Round each number to the same place. Add.

$$
\begin{array}{r}
3{,}6\,8\,0 \to 4{,}000 \\
+2{,}3\,2\,0 \to +2{,}000 \\
\hline
6{,}000
\end{array}
$$

Each number is rounded to the thousands place.

PRACTICE

Estimate the sums.

	a	b	c	d
1.	$544 \to 500$ $+233 \to +200$ 700	$373 \to$ $+519 \to$	$450 \to$ $+642 \to$	$841 \to$ $+790 \to$
2.	$516 \to 500$ $+6{,}724 \to +6{,}700$	$4{,}332 \to$ $+\ 789 \to$	$53{,}500 \to$ $+\ \ 284 \to$	$4{,}325 \to$ $+534{,}643 \to$
3.	$8{,}583 \to 9{,}000$ $+2{,}393 \to +2{,}000$	$4{,}325 \to$ $+7{,}543 \to$	$6{,}436 \to$ $+8{,}964 \to$	$8{,}975 \to$ $+9{,}633 \to$
4.	$97{,}905 \to 98{,}000$ $+\ 6{,}284 \to +\ 6{,}000$	$53{,}577 \to$ $+\ 6{,}743 \to$	$89{,}355 \to$ $+\ 3{,}678 \to$	$34{,}887 \to$ $+\ \ \ 646 \to$
5.	$54{,}363 \to 50{,}000$ $+64{,}918 \to +60{,}000$	$32{,}956 \to$ $+65{,}970 \to$	$43{,}343 \to$ $+79{,}064 \to$	$64{,}784 \to$ $+95{,}543 \to$

Estimation of Differences

To estimate a difference, first round each number to the same place. Then subtract the rounded numbers.

Estimate: 39,465 − 442

Round each number to the same place. Subtract.

$$
\begin{array}{r}
3\,9{,}4\,6\,5 \rightarrow 39{,}500 \\
-\quad 4\,4\,2 \rightarrow -\quad 400 \\
\hline
39{,}100
\end{array}
$$

Each number is rounded to the hundreds place.

Estimate: 8641 − 5322

Round each number to the same place. Subtract.

$$
\begin{array}{r}
8{,}6\,4\,1 \rightarrow 9{,}000 \\
-5{,}3\,2\,2 \rightarrow -5{,}000 \\
\hline
4{,}000
\end{array}
$$

Each number is rounded to the thousands place.

PRACTICE

Estimate the differences.

	a	b	c	d
1.	563 → 600 −265 → −300 300	895 → −435 →	865 → −657 →	975 → −864 →
2.	1,322 → 1,300 − 124 → − 100	7,657 → − 153 →	65,434 → − 654 →	18,764 → − 643 →
3.	5,902 → 6,000 −2,932 → −3,000	7,774 → −6,976 →	9,342 → −7,643 →	8,964 → −4,086 →
4.	53,864 → 54,000 − 896 → − 1,000	14,535 → −2,356 →	74,543 → − 4,864 →	49,564 → − 7,534 →
5.	43,865 → 40,000 −25,157 → −30,000	68,865 → −42,975 →	88,658 → − 5,970 →	98,221 → −34,657 →

Problem-Solving Strategy: Guess & Check

Thomas Jefferson was the sixth youngest person to sign the Declaration of Independence in 1776. Benjamin Franklin was 37 years older than Jefferson. The sum of their ages was 103. How old was Jefferson when he signed the Declaration of Independence?

Understand the problem.

- **What do you want to know?**
  Jefferson's age when he signed the Declaration of Independence

- **What information is given?**
  Clue 1: Jefferson's age + 37 = Franklin's age
  Clue 2: Jefferson's age + Franklin's age = 103

Plan how to solve it.

- **What strategy can you use?**
  You can guess an answer that satisfies the first clue.
  Then check to see if your answer satisfies the second clue.

Solve it.

- **How can you use this strategy to solve the problem?**
  Try to guess in an organized way so that each of your guesses gets closer to the exact answer. Use a table.

Guess Jefferson's Age	Check Clue 1	Clue 2	Evaluate the Guess
30	30 + 37 = 67	30 + 67 = 97	too low
40	40 + 37 = 77	40 + 77 = 117	too high
35	35 + 37 = 72	35 + 72 = 107	too high
34	34 + 37 = 71	34 + 71 = 105	too high
33	33 + 37 = 70	33 + 70 = 103	satisfies both clues

- **What is the answer?**
  Thomas Jefferson was 33 years old when he signed the Declaration of Independence.

Look back and check your answer.

- **Is your answer reasonable?**
  You can check addition with subtraction.

  70 − 37 = 33
  103 − 70 = 33

  The addition checks and the age satisfies both clues.
  The answer is reasonable.

Use guess and check to solve each problem.

1. Aaron is 1 year younger than Laura. The sum of their ages is 23 years. How old is each of them?

   Answer _____

2. Alan has seven United States coins. Their total value is 61 cents. What coins and how many of each does he have?

   Answer _____

3. A millipede has 14 more legs than a caterpillar. Together they have 46 legs. How many legs does a caterpillar have?

   Answer _____

4. Combined, the movies *Titanic* and *Gone with the Wind* won 19 Academy Awards. *Titanic* won 3 more awards than *Gone with the Wind*. How many awards did each movie win?

   Answer _____

5. "Superman The Escape" and "Desperado" are the two fastest roller coasters. The sum of their speeds is 180 miles per hour. "Superman" is 20 mph faster than "Desperado." How fast is each roller coaster?

   Answer _____

6. Nicole did an aerobics class and a yoga class for a total of 1 hour and 10 minutes. The yoga class was 30 minutes longer than the aerobics class. How long was each class?

   Answer _____

Problem-Solving Applications

Solve.

1. Eduardo bought a jacket for $79. He gave the cashier $100. How much change did he receive?

    Answer _____

2. Ally had 275 apple trees in her orchard. This year she planted 75 more. How many apple trees are in the orchard now?

    Answer _____

3. Lake Superior covers 31,820 square miles. Lake Huron covers 23,010 square miles. How much larger is Lake Superior than Lake Huron?

    Answer _____

4. From 1896–1996, the United States won 833 gold, 634 silver, and 548 bronze Olympic medals. How many medals did the U.S. win altogether?

    Answer _____

5. In one year, Canada produced 6,662 cars a day. Japan produced 27,933 cars a day. Estimate the number of cars they produced each day altogether.

    Answer _____

6. The diameter of the sun is 864,930 miles. The diameter of the moon is 2,156 miles. Estimate the difference in their diameters.

    Answer _____

7. Ken lives in Boston. His sister lives 296 miles away in Philadelphia. How many miles will he travel round-trip when he visits her?

    Answer _____

8. In one year, 93,872 people attended the Rose Bowl. That is 7,347 fewer people than attended the year before. How many people went to the Rose Bowl that year?

    Answer _____

Multiplication of 1-digit Numbers

To multiply by 1-digit numbers, use basic multiplication facts.

Find: 2 × 806

Multiply 6 by 2 ones. Regroup.	Multiply 0 by 2 ones. Regroup.	Multiply 800 by 2 ones.

```
  Th  H | T | O          Th  H | T | O          Th  H | T | O
          1                       1              1           1
      8   0   6               8   0   6               8   0   6
  ×           2           ×           2           ×           2
              2               1   2           1,  6   1   2
```

PRACTICE

Multiply.

	a	*b*	*c*	*d*

1.
```
   H  T  O        H  T  O        H  T  O        H  T  O
   3  4
      4  5           1  3           2  4           3  5
   ×     8        ×     3        ×     9        ×     5
   3  6  0
```

2.
```
   1 4 5          6 0 1          7 6 4          9 4 2
   ×   6          ×   3          ×   7          ×   8
```

3.
```
   4,3 6 2        6,0 4 8        2,6 1 5        7,8 4 3
   ×     5        ×     4        ×     9        ×     2
```

4.
```
   9 2,0 7 5      1 7,4 6 9      3 9,0 2 6      4 0,8 1 0
   ×       8      ×       5      ×       6      ×       7
```

Line up the digits. Then find the products.

	a	*b*	*c*

5. 573 × 3 = _____   576 × 4 = _____   3,425 × 6 = _____

```
   573
   ×  3
```

Zeros in Multiplication

When you multiply by tens, you need to write a zero as a **place holder**.

Remember,

- the product of 0 and any number is 0.
- the sum of 0 and any number is that number.

Find: 30 × 58

Multiply by 0 ones.	Write a zero place holder. Multiply by 3 tens. Regroup.	Add the partial products.
Th H T O 5 8 × 3 0 0 0	Th H T O 2 5 8 × 3 0 0 0 1, 7 4 0	Th H T O 5 8 × 3 0 0 0 + 1, 7 4 0 1, 7 4 0

PRACTICE

Multiply.

	a	b	c	d
1.	H T O 2 2 × 4 0 0 0 + 8 8 0 8 8 0	Th H T O 5 7 × 8 0	Th H T O 6 3 × 7 0	Th H T O 8 4 × 6 0
2.	3 0 × 4 0 0 0 + 1, 2 0 0 1, 2 0 0	7 0 × 6 0	5 8 0 × 3 0	4, 0 0 6 × 5 0

Line up the digits. Then find the products.

          a   b   c

3. $430 \times 70 = $ _____ $2{,}470 \times 90 = $ _____ $3{,}000 \times 80 = $ _____

     430
    × 70

Multiplication of 2-digit Numbers

To multiply by 2-digit numbers, multiply by the ones first. Then multiply by the tens. Then add these two **partial products.**

Find: 38 × 42

Multiply by 2 ones. Regroup.	Write a zero place holder. Multiply by 4 tens.	Add the partial products.
Th H T O 　　 1 　　 3 8 ×　 4 2 　　 7 6	Th H T O 　　 3 　　 3 8 ×　 4 2 　　 7 6 1, 5 2 0	Th H T O 　　 3 8 ×　 4 2 　　 7 6 + 1, 5 2 0 　 1, 5 9 6

PRACTICE

Multiply.

	a	b	c	d
1.	Th H T O 　 5 3 × 1 9 　 4 7 7 + 5 3 0 1, 0 0 7	Th H T O 　 8 9 × 4 6	Th H T O 　 7 6 × 8 5	TTh Th H T O 　 2 4 × 7 2
2.	5 6 7 × 3 4	3 2 0 × 7 5	8 1 6 × 3 9	9 2 6 × 4 5
3.	1, 5 4 3 × 5 3	2, 6 5 0 × 9 7	2, 5 0 1 × 2 8	3 4, 6 0 3 × 3 5

Line up the digits. Then find the products.

　　　　　　　　a　　　　　　　　　　　　b　　　　　　　　　　　　c

4. 457 × 31 = _____　　 2,506 × 94 = _____　　 20,463 × 83 = _____

　457
× 31

Multiplication of 3-digit Numbers

To multiply by 3-digit numbers, multiply by the ones first.
Then multiply by the tens and hundreds. Then add these
three partial products.

Find: 342 × 103

Multiply by 3 ones. Regroup.	Write a zero place holder. Multiply by 0 tens.	Write two zero place holders. Multiply by 1 hundred.	Add the partial products.

	Th	H	T	O
		1		
	3	4	2
×	1	0	3
1,	0	2	6

	Th	H	T	O
		3	4	2
×		1	0	3
1,	0	2	6
0	0	0	0

	TTh	Th	H	T	O
			3	4	2
×			1	0	3
	1,	0	2	6
	0	0	0	0
3	4,	2	0	0

	TTh	Th	H	T	O
			3	4	2
×			1	0	3
	1,	0	2	6
	0	0	0	0
+ 3	4,	2	0	0
3	5,	2	2	6

PRACTICE

Multiply.

	a	b	c	d
1.	361 ×313	358 ×637	507 ×383	870 ×647

$$
\begin{array}{r}
361 \\
\times 313 \\
\hline
1,083 \\
3,610 \\
+108,300 \\
\hline
112,993 \\
\end{array}
$$

	a	b	c	d
2.	950 ×603	621 ×583	932 ×785	400 ×803

Line up the digits. Then find the products.

       a   *b*   *c*

3. 783 × 342 = _____   850 × 330 = _____   742 × 582 = _____

$$
\begin{array}{r}
783 \\
\times 342 \\
\end{array}
$$

Estimation of Products

To estimate products, round each **factor.**
Then multiply the rounded factors.

Estimate: 72 × 35

Round each factor to the greatest place.
Multiply.

$$
\begin{array}{r}
7\,2 \rightarrow \quad 7\,0 \\
\times 3\,5 \rightarrow \times \quad 4\,0 \\
\hline
2,8\,0\,0
\end{array}
$$

Estimate: 369 × 21

Round each factor to the greatest place.
Multiply.

$$
\begin{array}{r}
3\,6\,9 \rightarrow \quad 4\,0\,0 \\
\times \quad 2\,1 \rightarrow \times \quad 2\,0 \\
\hline
8,0\,0\,0
\end{array}
$$

PRACTICE

Estimate the products.

	a	b	c	d
1.	$31 \rightarrow \;\; 30$ $\times 46 \rightarrow \times \;\; 50$ $\overline{1,500}$	$22 \rightarrow$ $\times 53 \rightarrow$	$74 \rightarrow$ $\times 55 \rightarrow$	$86 \rightarrow$ $\times 91 \rightarrow$
2.	$65 \rightarrow$ $\times 21 \rightarrow$	$47 \rightarrow$ $\times 32 \rightarrow$	$39 \rightarrow$ $\times 63 \rightarrow$	$59 \rightarrow$ $\times 77 \rightarrow$
3.	$54 \rightarrow$ $\times 41 \rightarrow$	$17 \rightarrow$ $\times 56 \rightarrow$	$62 \rightarrow$ $\times 89 \rightarrow$	$39 \rightarrow$ $\times 75 \rightarrow$
4.	$276 \rightarrow \;\; 300$ $\times \;\; 45 \rightarrow \times \;\; 50$ $\overline{15,000}$	$671 \rightarrow$ $\times \;\; 93 \rightarrow$	$253 \rightarrow$ $\times \;\; 85 \rightarrow$	$712 \rightarrow$ $\times \;\; 97 \rightarrow$

Line up the digits. Then estimate the products.

	a	b	c
5.	67 × 23 _____	94 × 52 _____	749 × 28 _____

$$
\begin{array}{r}
67 \rightarrow \;\; 70 \\
\times 23 \rightarrow \times 20 \\
\hline
\end{array}
$$

1-digit Divisors with Remainders

To divide by a 1-digit divisor, first choose a **trial quotient.**
Then multiply and subtract.

Remember, if your trial quotient is too large or too small,
try another number.

Find: 437 ÷ 8

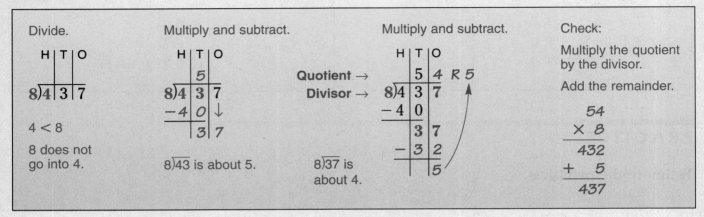

Divide.

```
  H|T|O
8)4|3|7
```
4 < 8

8 does not
go into 4.

Multiply and subtract.

```
    H|T|O
    |5|
8)4|3|7
 −4|0|↓
   |3|7
```
8)43 is about 5.

Multiply and subtract.

Quotient →
Divisor →
```
    |5|4  R 5
8)4|3|7
 −4|0|
   |3|7
  −|3|2
     |5
```
8)37 is
about 4.

Check:

Multiply the quotient
by the divisor.

Add the remainder.

```
    54
  ×  8
   432
  +  5
   437
```

PRACTICE

Divide.

      a   *b*   *c*   *d*

1.
```
  3 4 R1
2)6 9
 −6 ↓
   9
  −8
   1
```
        6)5 6 8   3)2 8 9   5)2 7 4

2.
  4)3, 3 8 5   9)8, 3 4 9   7)6, 8 9 3   8)4, 0 8 9

Set up the problems. Then find the quotients.

          a   *b*   *c*

3. 461 ÷ 3 = _____   784 ÷ 5 = _____   7,483 ÷ 9 = _____

3)461

Dividing by Multiples of 10

To divide by multiples of ten, choose a trial quotient.
Then multiply and subtract.

Find: 570 ÷ 40

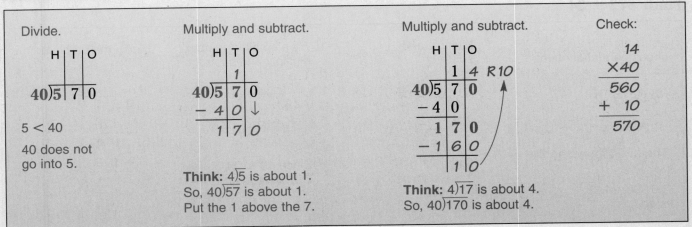

Divide.

H T O

40)5 7 0

5 < 40

40 does not
go into 5.

Multiply and subtract.

H T O
    1
40)5 7 0
− 4 0 ↓
    1 7 0

Think: 4)5 is about 1.
So, 40)57 is about 1.
Put the 1 above the 7.

Multiply and subtract.

H T O
    1 4 R10
40)5 7 0
− 4 0
    1 7 0
− 1 6 0
      1 0

Think: 4)17 is about 4.
So, 40)170 is about 4.

Check:
    14
  ×40
   560
 + 10
   570

PRACTICE

Divide.

        a   b   c   d

1.
        1 1 R 39
  40)4 7 9   80)4 3 0   20)3 6 8   10)4 9 7
   − 4 0 ↓
      7 9
    − 4 0
      3 9

2.
  50)6, 3 6 0   20)3, 8 5 6   40)5, 9 0 0   80)7, 8 5 0

Set up the problems. Then find the quotients.

            a   b   c

3. 3,875 ÷ 70 = _____   5,183 ÷ 20 = _____   6,032 ÷ 20 = _____

   70)3,875

Trial Quotient: Too Large or Too Small

When you divide, you may have to try several quotients. Use rounding to choose a trial quotient. Then multiply and subtract. If it is too large or too small, try again.

Find: 672 ÷ 24

Use rounding to choose a trial quotient.	Multiply and subtract.	Try a smaller number. Multiply and subtract.	Finish the problem.
$24\overline{)6\ 7\ 2}$	$\begin{array}{r} 3 \\ 24\overline{)6\ 7\ 2} \\ -7\ 2 \end{array}$	$\begin{array}{r} 2 \\ 24\overline{)6\ 7\ 2} \\ -4\ 8 \\ \hline 1\ 9 \end{array}$	$\begin{array}{r} 2\ 8 \\ 24\overline{)6\ 7\ 2} \\ -4\ 8\downarrow \\ \hline 1\ 9\ 2 \\ -1\ 9\ 2 \\ \hline 0 \end{array}$
Think: 24 rounds to 20. $\begin{array}{r} 3 \\ 2\overline{)6} \end{array}$ So, $24\overline{)67}$ is about 3.	Since 72 > 67, 3 is too large.	Since 19 < 24, 2 is correct.	

Find: 675 ÷ 15

$15\overline{)6\ 7\ 5}$	$\begin{array}{r} 3 \\ 15\overline{)6\ 7\ 5} \\ -4\ 5 \\ \hline 2\ 2 \end{array}$	$\begin{array}{r} 4 \\ 15\overline{)6\ 7\ 5} \\ -6\ 0 \\ \hline 7 \end{array}$	$\begin{array}{r} 4\ 5 \\ 15\overline{)6\ 7\ 5} \\ -6\ 0\downarrow \\ \hline 7\ 5 \\ -7\ 5 \\ \hline 0 \end{array}$
Think: 15 rounds to 20. $\begin{array}{r} 3 \\ 2\overline{)6} \end{array}$ So, $15\overline{)67}$ is about 3.	Since 22 > 15, 3 is too small.	Since 7 < 15, 4 is correct.	

PRACTICE

Write *too large, too small,* or *correct* for each trial quotient. Then write the correct trial quotient.

a   *b*

1. $\begin{array}{r} 2 \\ 25\overline{)4\ 7\ 5} \end{array}$ __too large__ __1__ $\begin{array}{r} 3 \\ 15\overline{)6\ 8\ 2} \end{array}$ _____

2. $\begin{array}{r} 4 \\ 61\overline{)2,4\ 1\ 9} \end{array}$ _____ $\begin{array}{r} 3 \\ 42\overline{)1,2\ 5\ 3} \end{array}$ _____

3. $\begin{array}{r} 8 \\ 54\overline{)4\ 1,2\ 4\ 9} \end{array}$ _____ $\begin{array}{r} 3 \\ 27\overline{)6\ 5,4\ 8\ 7} \end{array}$ _____

Zeros in Quotients

When you cannot divide, write a zero in the quotient as a place holder.

Find: 2,430 ÷ 4

Divide.	Multiply and subtract.	Multiply and subtract.	Multiply and subtract.

Divide.

```
 Th│H│T│O
4)2,│4│3│0
```
2 < 4

4 does not go into 2.

Multiply and subtract.

```
    Th│ H │T│O
       │ 6 │ │
   4)2,│ 4 │3│0
    − 2│ 4 │↓│
       │ 0 │3│
```

```
  6
4)24
```

Multiply and subtract.

```
    Th│ H │T │O
       │ 6 │ 0│      ← Write a zero
   4)2,│ 4 │ 3│0        in the quotient
    − 2│ 4 │ ↓│         as a place
       │ 0 │ 3│         holder.
       │ − │ 0│↓
       │   │ 3│0
```

```
  0
4)3
```

Multiply and subtract.

```
    Th│ H │T │O
       │ 6 │ 0│ 7  R 2
   4)2,│ 4 │ 3│ 0
    − 2│ 4 │ ↓│
       │ 0 │ 3│
       │ − │ 0│↓
       │   │ 3│ 0
       │   │− 2│ 8
       │   │   │ 2
```

PRACTICE

Divide.

	a	b	c	d

1.
```
      3 0 4
   2)6 0 8
    −6 ↓
     0 0
    −  0 ↓
       0 8
    −    8
         0
```

b.
```
4)4 2 8
```

c.
```
9)1,8 4 5
```

d.
```
7)1,4 6 3
```

2.
```
81)4 1,0 6 7
```

```
97)5 8,3 9 4
```

```
89)1 8,5 1 2
```

```
52)3 6,4 5 2
```

2-digit Divisors with Remainders

To divide by a 2-digit divisor, first choose a trial quotient.
Multiply and subtract. Then write the remainder in the quotient.

Find: 739 ÷ 22

Divide.	Multiply and subtract.	Multiply and subtract.	Check:

H T O
 	
22)7 3 9
 	
7 < 22
 	
22 does not
go into 7.
	H T O
	    3
	22)7 3 9
	  − 6 6 ↓
	  ───────
	      7 9
	
	2)7 is about 3.
	So, 22)73 is about 3.
		H T O
		    3 3 R 13
		22)7 3 9
		  − 6 6
		  ───────
		      7 9
		    − 6 6
		    ───────
		        1 3
		
		2)7 is about 3.
		So, 22)79 is about 3.
			33
			×22
			────
			726
			+ 13
			────
			739

PRACTICE

Divide.

       a   b   c   d

1.
```
      4 2 R 2
  15)6 3 2
  −6 0 ↓
  ──────
     3 2
   − 3 0
   ──────
       2
```
                      35)6 8 3   31)2 9 5   36)5 8 2

2.
27)4, 5 2 1   84)5, 9 3 4   41)5, 2 1 9   62)8, 6 9 4

3.
71)7 3, 5 1 2   12)3 2, 6 9 2   32)3 3, 1 7 4   57)4 2, 5 2 8

Estimation of Quotients

To estimate quotients, round the numbers to use basic division facts.

Estimate: 243 ÷ 5

Round the dividend to use a basic fact. Divide.

$5\overline{)243}$ 243 ÷ 5

Think: 25 ÷ 5 = 5   ↓   ↓

250 ÷ 5 = 50

Estimate: 424 ÷ 61

Round the dividend and the divisor to use a basic fact. Divide.

$61\overline{)424}$ 424 ÷ 61

Think: 42 ÷ 6 = 7   ↓   ↓

420 ÷ 60 = 7

PRACTICE

Round the dividends to estimate the quotients.

	a	b	c	d
1.	$3\overline{)1\ 3\ 1} \rightarrow 3\overline{)1\ 2\ 0}^{\ 4\ 0}$	$4\overline{)2\ 8\ 4} \rightarrow$	$8\overline{)7\ 1\ 2} \rightarrow$	$4\overline{)8\ 0\ 7} \rightarrow$
2.	$8\overline{)5,\ 7\ 4\ 7} \rightarrow$	$7\overline{)2,3\ 1\ 2} \rightarrow$	$5\overline{)2,9\ 3\ 4} \rightarrow$	$8\overline{)3,9\ 5\ 4} \rightarrow$

Round the dividends and the divisors to estimate the quotients.

	a	b	c	d
3.	$23\overline{)7\ 8\ 3} \rightarrow 20\overline{)8\ 0\ 0}^{\ 4\ 0}$	$35\overline{)8\ 0\ 5} \rightarrow$	$29\overline{)5\ 9\ 7} \rightarrow$	$43\overline{)2\ 8\ 9} \rightarrow$
4.	$42\overline{)8\ 0\ 7} \rightarrow$	$53\overline{)7\ 5\ 4} \rightarrow$	$84\overline{)6\ 4\ 4} \rightarrow$	$86\overline{)5\ 3\ 7} \rightarrow$

Problem-Solving Strategy: Choose an Operation

Pythons are the longest snakes in the world. The largest python was found in Indonesia in 1912. It was 396 inches long. Since there are 12 inches in 1 foot, how many feet long was the python?

Understand the problem.

- **What do you want to know?**
  the length of the python in feet

- **What information is given?**
  It was 396 inches long.
  There are 12 inches in 1 foot.

Plan how to solve it.

- **What strategy can you use?**
  You can choose the operation needed to solve it.

Add to combine unequal groups.	**Multiply** to combine equal groups.
Subtract to separate into unequal groups.	**Divide** to separate into equal groups.

Solve it.

- **How can you use this strategy to solve the problem?**
  Since you need to separate the total 396 inches into equal groups of 12 inches, you should divide to find *how many equal groups.*

$$\begin{array}{r} 33 \\ 12\overline{)396} \\ -36\downarrow \\ \hline 36 \\ -36 \\ \hline 0 \end{array}$$

- **What is the answer?**
  The python was 33 feet long.

Look back and check your answer.

- **Is your answer reasonable?**
  You can check division with multiplication.

$$\begin{array}{r} 33 \\ \times\ 12 \\ \hline 396 \end{array}$$

The product matches the dividend.
The answer is reasonable.

**Choose an operation to solve each problem.
Then solve the problem.**

1. There are 15 teams in the soccer league. Each team has 17 players. How many players are in the league altogether?

   Operation _____

   Answer _____

2. The average alligator is 180 inches long. How many feet long is an average alligator? (1 foot = 12 inches)

   Operation _____

   Answer _____

3. North Dakota covers 70,704 square miles. South Dakota covers 77,121 square miles. How much land do the Dakotas cover in all?

   Operation _____

   Answer _____

4. In 1967, 61,946 people attended the first Super Bowl. In 1968, 75,546 people attended. How many more people went to the second Super Bowl than the first?

   Operation _____

   Answer _____

5. It is 385 miles between San Francisco and Los Angeles. Driving at 55 miles per hour, how long will the trip take?

   Operation _____

   Answer _____

6. Charles worked 40 hours this week and made $520. How much did he earn each hour?

   Operation _____

   Answer _____

Problem-Solving Applications

Solve.

1. There are 4 performances of the school play this weekend. The theater seats 263 people. How many people can see the show this weekend?

   Answer _____

2. Fran's Market received 960 cans of soup. The cans arrived in 40 boxes. Each box held the same number of cans. How many cans were in each box?

   Answer _____

3. King Cobras are usually 156 inches long. What is the average length of a King Cobra in feet? (1 ft = 12 in.)

   Answer _____

4. Domingo ran 7 miles every day. How far did he run in all during the last 23 days?

   Answer _____

5. An apartment building has 28 floors. Each floor has 18 apartments. How many apartments are in the building?

   Answer _____

6. Each section of the stadium seats 275 people. There are 115 sections. How many people can the entire stadium seat?

   Answer _____

7. A total of 158 students went on the Aquarium trip. They took 4 busses. Estimate how many students were on each bus.

   Answer _____

8. Jake's Bakery sold 564 pies last week for $17 each. Estimate the total amount of money the bakery collected for pies last week.

   Answer _____

Unit 1 Whole Numbers and Operations

Write the place name for the 7 in each number.

      a   *b*

1. 67,302,284 _____   528,972,343 _____

Write each number using digits. Insert commas where needed.

2. one million, fifty thousand, forty-five _____

3. two million, seven thousand, six _____

Compare. Write <, >, or =.

   a   *b*   *c*

4. 590 _____ 462   57,098 _____ 650,245   1,202,865 _____ 36,248,762

Write in order from least to greatest.

5. 702   722   720 _____

6. 6,789   9,789   9,786 _____

Add or subtract.

	a	*b*	*c*	*d*
7.	542 + 21	934 −547	99,247 −75,421	35,798 + 465
8.	4,532 + 532	9,964 −4,345	8,684 −2,343	864 +155
9.	589,321 −257,432	89,492 54,982 +42,568	534,975 −238,573	374,920 586,483 +732,109

Estimate the sums or differences.

	a	*b*	*c*
10.	54 → +562 →	453 → −298 →	764 → +234 →
11.	32,342 → +76,964 →	72,432 → −45,864 →	1,155 → +25,677 →

UNIT 1 Review

Multiply.

	a	b	c	d

12.
$$\begin{array}{r} 4\ 6 \\ \times\quad 3 \\ \hline \end{array} \qquad \begin{array}{r} 4\ 7 \\ \times\quad 4 \\ \hline \end{array} \qquad \begin{array}{r} 3\ 4\ 4 \\ \times\qquad 6 \\ \hline \end{array} \qquad \begin{array}{r} 8\ 9 \\ \times 5\ 6 \\ \hline \end{array}$$

13.
$$\begin{array}{r} 4\ 6\ 8 \\ \times\quad 2\ 5 \\ \hline \end{array} \qquad \begin{array}{r} 6\ 3\ 7 \\ \times\quad 7\ 5 \\ \hline \end{array} \qquad \begin{array}{r} 8,5\ 4\ 4 \\ \times\qquad 3\ 4 \\ \hline \end{array} \qquad \begin{array}{r} 3\ 4,8\ 6\ 4 \\ \times\qquad\quad 5\ 0 \\ \hline \end{array}$$

14.
$$\begin{array}{r} 5\ 3,0\ 5\ 6 \\ \times\qquad\quad 3\ 5 \\ \hline \end{array} \qquad \begin{array}{r} 5\ 0\ 6 \\ \times 7\ 6\ 3 \\ \hline \end{array} \qquad \begin{array}{r} 5\ 5\ 3 \\ \times 6\ 0\ 2 \\ \hline \end{array} \qquad \begin{array}{r} 9\ 0\ 0 \\ \times 5\ 0\ 0 \\ \hline \end{array}$$

Divide.

	a	b	c	d

15. $8\overline{)6\ 7\ 5}$ $4\overline{)8\ 9\ 0}$ $6\overline{)7,6\ 5\ 3}$ $5\overline{)6\ 7,0\ 4\ 5}$

16. $3\ 4\overline{)7\ 5\ 8}$ $6\ 0\overline{)5\ 7\ 3}$ $2\ 6\overline{)5,7\ 0\ 0}$ $7\ 0\overline{)8,4\ 0\ 2}$

17. $3\ 4\overline{)8\ 6,4\ 6\ 5}$ $8\ 3\overline{)6\ 4,9\ 0\ 8}$ $8\ 0\overline{)5\ 6,3\ 9\ 6}$ $5\ 1\overline{)7\ 6,9\ 9\ 8}$

Estimate the products or quotients.

	a	b	c

18.
$$\begin{array}{r} 5\ 7 \rightarrow \\ \times 7\ 9 \rightarrow \\ \hline \end{array} \qquad 8\overline{)4\ 3\ 5} \rightarrow \qquad \begin{array}{r} 7\ 6 \rightarrow \\ \times 2\ 1 \rightarrow \\ \hline \end{array}$$

19. $7\overline{)5,6\ 3\ 2} \rightarrow$ $\begin{array}{r} 6\ 8\ 3 \rightarrow \\ \times\quad 4\ 9 \rightarrow \\ \hline \end{array}$ $8\ 1\overline{)3\ 4\ 5} \rightarrow$

Use guess and check to solve each problem.

20. Shawn and Andy made 86 cupcakes in all. Shawn made 10 more than Andy. How many cupcakes did they each make?

Answer _____

21. Gail has eight United States coins. Their total value is 93 cents. What coins does she have?

Answer _____

Choose an operation to solve each problem. Then solve the problem.

22. John has 123 more baseball cards than Mark. Mark has 679 cards. How many baseball cards does John have?

Operation _____

Answer _____

23. Judy earns $390 a week. She works 30 hours per week. How much does she make each hour?

Operation _____

Answer _____

24. There were 1,291 cars in the parking lot this morning. By 5:00 P.M., 138 cars had left. How many cars were still in the parking lot?

Operation _____

Answer _____

25. The *Daily News* packs 458 bundles of newspapers every day. Each bundle has 250 papers. How many papers does the *Daily News* pack each day?

Operation _____

Answer _____

Meaning of Fractions

A **fraction** names part of a whole. This circle has
4 equal parts. Each part is $\frac{1}{4}$ of the circle.

Three of the equal parts are shaded blue.

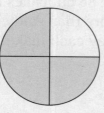

numerator

$\underset{\text{denominator}}{\overset{\text{numerator}}{\dfrac{3}{4}}}$ — three blue parts
— four parts in all

We read $\frac{3}{4}$ as three fourths.

A fraction also names parts of a group.
Two of the five squares are shaded blue.

$\dfrac{2}{5}$ — two blue squares
— five squares in all

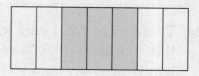

Two fifths are blue.

PRACTICE

Write the fraction and the word name for the part that is shaded.

        a   *b*   *c*

1.

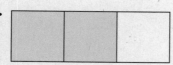   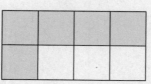   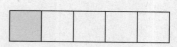

$\frac{2}{3}$ or *two thirds*   _____ or _____   _____ or _____

2.

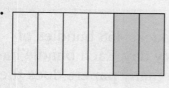   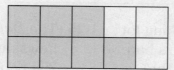

_____ or _____   _____ or _____   _____ or _____

Write the fraction for the word name.

        a   *b*   *c*

3. three eighths $\frac{3}{8}$ one fourth _____   four fifths _____

Write the word name for the fraction.

        a   *b*   *c*

4. $\frac{5}{6}$ *five sixths* $\frac{2}{7}$ _____ $\frac{7}{8}$ _____

Improper Fractions and Mixed Numbers

An **improper fraction** is a fraction with a numerator that is greater than or equal to the denominator.

$\frac{6}{6}$, $\frac{12}{3}$, and $\frac{8}{5}$ are improper fractions.

An improper fraction can be written as a whole or mixed number.

A **mixed number** is a whole number and a fraction.

$1\frac{3}{4}$ is a mixed number.

A mixed number can be written as an improper fraction.

Write $\frac{6}{6}$ and $\frac{12}{3}$ as whole numbers.

Divide the numerator by the denominator.

$$6\overline{)6}^{\ 1} \qquad \frac{6}{6} = 1$$

$$3\overline{)12}^{\ 4} \qquad \frac{12}{3} = 4$$

Write $\frac{8}{5}$ as a mixed number.

Divide the numerator by the denominator. Write the remainder as a fraction by writing the remainder over the divisor.

$$5\overline{)8}^{\ 1\frac{3}{5}}$$
$$\underline{-5}$$
$$3$$

$$\frac{8}{5} = 1\frac{3}{5}$$

Write $1\frac{3}{4}$ as an improper fraction.

Multiply the whole number by the denominator. Add this product to the numerator. Then write the sum over the denominator.

$$1\frac{3}{4} = \frac{1 \times 4 + 3}{4} = \frac{4 + 3}{4} = \frac{7}{4}$$

$$1\frac{3}{4} = \frac{7}{4}$$

PRACTICE

Write as a whole number.

	a	b	c	d
1.	$\frac{16}{4} = \underline{\quad 4 \quad}$	$\frac{15}{5} = \underline{\qquad}$	$\frac{18}{3} = \underline{\qquad}$	$\frac{24}{8} = \underline{\qquad}$
2.	$\frac{36}{9} = \underline{\qquad}$	$\frac{28}{4} = \underline{\qquad}$	$\frac{48}{6} = \underline{\qquad}$	$\frac{25}{25} = \underline{\qquad}$

Write as a mixed number.

	a	b	c	d
3.	$\frac{15}{4} = \underline{\quad 3\frac{3}{4} \quad}$	$\frac{21}{5} = \underline{\qquad}$	$\frac{14}{3} = \underline{\qquad}$	$\frac{27}{4} = \underline{\qquad}$
4.	$\frac{23}{6} = \underline{\qquad}$	$\frac{12}{7} = \underline{\qquad}$	$\frac{35}{8} = \underline{\qquad}$	$\frac{7}{2} = \underline{\qquad}$

Write as an improper fraction.

	a	b	c	d
5.	$2\frac{7}{10} = \underline{\quad \frac{27}{10} \quad}$	$8\frac{1}{2} = \underline{\qquad}$	$7\frac{2}{3} = \underline{\qquad}$	$3\frac{2}{5} = \underline{\qquad}$
6.	$8\frac{1}{3} = \underline{\qquad}$	$5\frac{1}{6} = \underline{\qquad}$	$6\frac{1}{4} = \underline{\qquad}$	$2\frac{7}{8} = \underline{\qquad}$

Equivalent Fractions

To add or subtract fractions, you might need to use
equivalent fractions, or fractions that have the same value.

To change a fraction to an equivalent fraction in **higher terms,**
multiply the numerator and the denominator by the same number.

Rewrite $\frac{3}{4}$ with 8 as the denominator.

Compare the denominators.	Multiply both the numerator and the denominator by 2.
$\frac{3}{4} = \frac{}{8}$ Think: $4 \times 2 = 8$	$\frac{3}{4} = \frac{3 \times 2}{4 \times 2} = \frac{6}{8}$

You can also use the **lowest common denominator** (LCD)
to write equivalent fractions.

Use the LCD to write equivalent fractions for $\frac{1}{2}$ and $\frac{2}{5}$.

List several multiples for each denominator.	Find the LCD. It is the smallest number that appears on both lists.	Write equivalent fractions.
Multiples of 2: 2 4 6 8 10 12 **Multiples of 5:** 5 10 15 20 25	The LCD of $\frac{1}{2}$ and $\frac{2}{5}$ is 10.	$\frac{1}{2} = \frac{1 \times 5}{2 \times 5} = \frac{5}{10}$ $\frac{2}{5} = \frac{2 \times 2}{5 \times 2} = \frac{4}{10}$

PRACTICE

Rewrite each fraction as an equivalent fraction in higher terms.

	a	b	c	d
1.	$\frac{5}{8} = \frac{5 \times 2}{8 \times 2} = \frac{10}{16}$	$\frac{3}{4} = \frac{}{16}$	$\frac{2}{3} = \frac{}{12}$	$\frac{2}{5} = \frac{}{10}$
2.	$\frac{3}{5} = \frac{}{25}$	$\frac{2}{5} = \frac{}{15}$	$\frac{5}{6} = \frac{}{24}$	$\frac{7}{8} = \frac{}{16}$

Use the LCD to write equivalent fractions.

	a	b	c	d
3.	$\frac{1}{3} = \frac{1 \times 2}{3 \times 2} = \frac{2}{6}$	$\frac{1}{2} =$	$\frac{7}{10} =$	$\frac{2}{3} =$
	$\frac{1}{2} = \frac{1 \times 3}{2 \times 3} = \frac{3}{6}$	$\frac{3}{5} =$	$\frac{3}{4} =$	$\frac{5}{7} =$
4.	$\frac{7}{8} =$	$\frac{1}{4} =$	$\frac{4}{5} =$	$\frac{1}{6} =$
	$\frac{5}{6} =$	$\frac{2}{5} =$	$\frac{1}{3} =$	$\frac{3}{4} =$

Simplifying Fractions

When you find the answer to a problem with fractions, you might need to change the fraction to an equivalent fraction in simplest terms. To **simplify** a fraction, divide both the numerator and the denominator by the same greatest number possible.

Simplify: $\frac{8}{14}$

Consider the numerator and denominator.	Divide the numerator and the denominator by 2.
$\frac{8}{14} =$ **Think:** 14 can be divided by 7 but 8 cannot. 8 can be divided by 4 but 14 cannot. Both 14 and 8 can be divided by 2.	$\frac{8}{14} = \frac{8 \div 2}{14 \div 2} = \frac{4}{7}$

A fraction is in simplest terms when 1 is the only number that divides both the numerator and the denominator evenly.

The fraction $\frac{4}{7}$ is in simplest terms.

PRACTICE

Simplify.

	a	b	c	d
1.	$\frac{9}{21} = \frac{9 \div 3}{21 \div 3} = \frac{3}{7}$	$\frac{2}{10} =$	$\frac{4}{12} =$	$\frac{12}{18} =$
2.	$\frac{4}{6} =$	$\frac{2}{8} =$	$\frac{8}{20} =$	$\frac{10}{12} =$
3.	$\frac{45}{45} =$	$\frac{9}{15} =$	$\frac{2}{12} =$	$\frac{6}{14} =$
4.	$\frac{9}{12} =$	$\frac{3}{9} =$	$\frac{10}{20} =$	$\frac{6}{8} =$
5.	$\frac{10}{25} =$	$\frac{8}{10} =$	$\frac{14}{16} =$	$\frac{5}{15} =$
6.	$\frac{9}{21} =$	$\frac{2}{20} =$	$\frac{4}{36} =$	$\frac{12}{24} =$

Addition and Subtraction of Fractions with Like Denominators

To add or subtract fractions with like denominators, add or subtract the numerators. Use the same denominator. Simplify the answer.

Remember,

- to simplify an improper fraction, write it as a whole number or a mixed number.

- to simplify a proper fraction, write it in simplest terms.

Find: $\frac{9}{10} + \frac{8}{10}$

Add the numerators.	Use the same denominator.
$\begin{array}{r} \frac{9}{10} \\ +\frac{8}{10} \\ \hline 17 \end{array}$	$\begin{array}{r} \frac{9}{10} \\ +\frac{8}{10} \\ \hline \frac{17}{10} = 1\frac{7}{10} \end{array}$
Simplify the answer.	

Find: $\frac{11}{12} - \frac{7}{12}$

Subtract the numerators.	Use the same denominator.
$\begin{array}{r} \frac{11}{12} \\ -\frac{7}{12} \\ \hline 4 \end{array}$	$\begin{array}{r} \frac{11}{12} \\ -\frac{7}{12} \\ \hline \frac{4}{12} = \frac{1}{3} \end{array}$
Simplify the answer.	

PRACTICE

Add. Simplify.

	a	b	c	d	e
1.	$\frac{3}{8}$ $+\frac{1}{8}$ $\frac{4}{8} = \frac{1}{2}$	$\frac{3}{10}$ $+\frac{1}{10}$	$\frac{2}{6}$ $+\frac{1}{6}$	$\frac{5}{16}$ $+\frac{1}{16}$	$\frac{7}{16}$ $+\frac{3}{16}$
2.	$\frac{5}{6}$ $+\frac{2}{6}$ $\frac{7}{6} = 1\frac{1}{6}$	$\frac{7}{8}$ $+\frac{5}{8}$	$\frac{8}{10}$ $+\frac{5}{10}$	$\frac{4}{5}$ $+\frac{3}{5}$	$\frac{11}{12}$ $+\frac{6}{12}$

Subtract. Simplify.

	a	b	c	d	e
3.	$\frac{5}{8}$ $-\frac{3}{8}$ $\frac{2}{8} = \frac{1}{4}$	$\frac{7}{10}$ $-\frac{3}{10}$	$\frac{7}{12}$ $-\frac{5}{12}$	$\frac{5}{8}$ $-\frac{1}{8}$	$\frac{15}{16}$ $-\frac{3}{16}$

Addition of Fractions with Different Denominators

To add fractions with different denominators, first rewrite the fractions as equivalent fractions with like denominators. Then add the numerators and simplify the answer.

Find: $\frac{1}{6} + \frac{1}{3}$

Write equivalent fractions with like denominators.		Add the numerators. Use the same denominator.
$\begin{array}{r} \frac{1}{6} = \frac{1}{6} \\ +\frac{1}{3} = \frac{2}{6} \\ \hline \end{array}$	Remember, $\frac{1}{3} = \frac{1 \times 2}{3 \times 2} = \frac{2}{6}$	$\begin{array}{r} \frac{1}{6} = \frac{1}{6} \\ +\frac{1}{3} = \frac{2}{6} \\ \hline \frac{3}{6} = \frac{1}{2} \end{array}$ Simplify the answer.

PRACTICE

Add. Simplify.

	a	b	c	d
1.	$\begin{array}{r} \frac{1}{5} = \frac{2}{10} \\ +\frac{1}{10} = \frac{1}{10} \\ \hline \frac{3}{10} \end{array}$	$\begin{array}{r} \frac{1}{4} \\ +\frac{1}{2} \\ \hline \end{array}$	$\begin{array}{r} \frac{1}{2} \\ +\frac{3}{8} \\ \hline \end{array}$	$\begin{array}{r} \frac{3}{4} \\ +\frac{1}{8} \\ \hline \end{array}$
2.	$\begin{array}{r} \frac{3}{4} = \frac{9}{12} \\ +\frac{1}{12} = \frac{1}{12} \\ \hline \frac{10}{12} = \frac{5}{6} \end{array}$	$\begin{array}{r} \frac{1}{2} \\ +\frac{1}{6} \\ \hline \end{array}$	$\begin{array}{r} \frac{1}{10} \\ +\frac{1}{2} \\ \hline \end{array}$	$\begin{array}{r} \frac{5}{12} \\ +\frac{1}{4} \\ \hline \end{array}$
3.	$\begin{array}{r} \frac{1}{2} = \frac{5}{10} \\ +\frac{3}{10} = \frac{3}{10} \\ \hline \frac{8}{10} = \frac{4}{5} \end{array}$	$\begin{array}{r} \frac{5}{16} \\ +\frac{1}{4} \\ \hline \end{array}$	$\begin{array}{r} \frac{1}{2} \\ +\frac{5}{12} \\ \hline \end{array}$	$\begin{array}{r} \frac{4}{9} \\ +\frac{1}{3} \\ \hline \end{array}$

Set up the problems. Then find the sums. Simplify.

	a	b	c
4.	$\frac{1}{3} + \frac{2}{9} =$ _____	$\frac{2}{8} + \frac{1}{24} =$ _____	$\frac{3}{6} + \frac{2}{18} =$ _____

$$\begin{array}{r} \frac{1}{3} \\ +\frac{2}{9} \\ \hline \end{array}$$

Addition of Fractions Using the Least Common Denominator

Find: $\frac{1}{2} + \frac{3}{5}$

Write equivalent fractions with like denominators. Use the LCD.	Add the numerators. Use the same denominator.
$\frac{1}{2} = \frac{1 \times 5}{2 \times 5} = \frac{5}{10}$ $+\frac{3}{5} = \frac{3 \times 2}{5 \times 2} = \frac{6}{10}$	$\frac{1}{2} = \frac{5}{10}$ $+\frac{3}{5} = \frac{6}{10}$ $\frac{11}{10} = 1\frac{1}{10}$ Simplify the answer.

GUIDED PRACTICE

Add. Simplify.

	a	b	c	d
1.	$\frac{1}{2} = \frac{3}{6}$ $+\frac{2}{3} = \frac{4}{6}$ $\frac{7}{6} = 1\frac{1}{6}$	$\frac{3}{7}$ $+\frac{1}{2}$	$\frac{2}{3}$ $+\frac{3}{4}$	$\frac{2}{5}$ $+\frac{7}{9}$
2.	$\frac{2}{3}$ $+\frac{7}{8}$	$\frac{3}{8}$ $+\frac{5}{6}$	$\frac{4}{5}$ $+\frac{2}{3}$	$\frac{2}{7}$ $+\frac{2}{3}$
3.	$\frac{5}{6}$ $+\frac{3}{4}$	$\frac{1}{3}$ $+\frac{3}{10}$	$\frac{5}{6}$ $+\frac{3}{5}$	$\frac{1}{2}$ $+\frac{5}{9}$

Set up the problems. Then find the sums. Simplify.

a
4. $\frac{3}{7} + \frac{1}{4} = $ _____

$\frac{3}{7}$
$+\frac{1}{4}$

b
$\frac{4}{5} + \frac{7}{11} = $ _____

c
$\frac{1}{7} + \frac{2}{8} = $ _____

PRACTICE

Add. Simplify.

	a	*b*	*c*	*d*
1.	$\frac{1}{5}$ $+\frac{1}{2}$	$\frac{5}{12}$ $+\frac{1}{4}$	$\frac{5}{6}$ $+\frac{1}{4}$	$\frac{2}{3}$ $+\frac{1}{6}$
2.	$\frac{5}{8}$ $+\frac{1}{7}$	$\frac{2}{3}$ $+\frac{3}{4}$	$\frac{5}{7}$ $+\frac{1}{2}$	$\frac{4}{9}$ $+\frac{1}{6}$
3.	$\frac{3}{4}$ $+\frac{2}{10}$	$\frac{3}{8}$ $+\frac{2}{9}$	$\frac{4}{5}$ $+\frac{3}{20}$	$\frac{1}{3}$ $+\frac{6}{18}$

Set up the problems. Then find the sums. Simplify.

        a   *b*   *c*

4. $\frac{3}{8} + \frac{2}{12} =$ _____ $\frac{5}{7} + \frac{1}{3} =$ _____ $\frac{6}{9} + \frac{3}{12} =$ _____

MIXED PRACTICE

Find each answer.

	a	*b*	*c*	*d*
1.	$\begin{array}{r} 3\,9\,8 \\ +7\,5\,4 \end{array}$	$\begin{array}{r} 7\,0\,3 \\ -1\,9\,9 \end{array}$	$\begin{array}{r} 4\,5,4\,3\,3 \\ -2\,8,6\,9\,5 \end{array}$	$\begin{array}{r} 1\,0\,7,9\,6\,3 \\ +\ \ 6\,9,3\,3\,2 \end{array}$
2.	$\begin{array}{r} 9,2\,1\,0 \\ \times\ \ \ \ \ 8 \end{array}$	$6\overline{)1,4\,8\,2}$	$\begin{array}{r} 5\,4\,3 \\ \times\ \ 2\,1 \end{array}$	$4\overline{)3,8\,2\,0}$

Problem-Solving Strategy: Make a Graph

Coach Esteves took a survey to choose the team's mascot. Of the 24 players, $\frac{1}{3}$ chose Bulldogs, $\frac{1}{2}$ chose Bears, and $\frac{1}{6}$ chose Lions. How can he present the results of the survey to the team?

Understand the problem.

- **What do you want to know?**
  how to present the results of the survey

- **What information is given?**
  24 people voted: $\frac{1}{3}$ for Bulldogs, $\frac{1}{2}$ for Bears, and $\frac{1}{6}$ for Lions.

Plan how to solve it.

- **What strategy can you use?**
  You can make a circle graph to show the data as parts of a whole.

Solve it.

- **How can you use this strategy to solve the problem?**
  Use a circle divided into 24 equal parts to represent the whole team. Then shade and label the number of votes for each mascot. (Remember, to find $\frac{1}{2}$ of 8, divide 8 by 2. $\frac{1}{2}$ of $8 = 8 \div 2 = 4$)

Mascot	Fraction of All the Votes	Number of Votes
Bulldogs	$\frac{1}{3}$ of 24 =	8
Bears	$\frac{1}{2}$ of 24 =	12
Lions	$\frac{1}{6}$ of 24 =	4

TEAM MASCOT VOTE

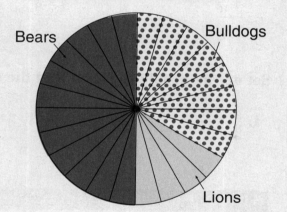

- **What is the answer?**
  The results of the survey can be presented in a circle graph.

Look back and check your answer.

- **Is your answer reasonable?**
  The whole circle represents the whole survey—24 votes.
  The sum of the number of votes in each section should be 24.

  $8 + 12 + 4 = 24$

  The answer is reasonable.

Make a graph to solve each problem.

1. Jamal has 28 CDs in his collection. $\frac{1}{4}$ of the CDs are Rock, $\frac{1}{2}$ are R&B, and $\frac{1}{4}$ are Jazz. Make a circle graph to show Jamal's CD collection.

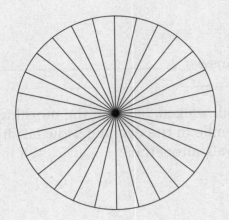

2. Twelve students voted for their favorite ice cream. Vanilla got $\frac{1}{6}$ of the votes, chocolate got $\frac{2}{3}$, and strawberry got $\frac{1}{6}$. Make a circle graph to show the results of the vote.

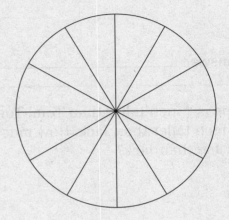

3. Laura worked 8 hours today. She spent $\frac{1}{2}$ the time in meetings, $\frac{1}{8}$ on the phone, and the rest of the time on the computer. Make a circle graph to show how Laura spent her work day.

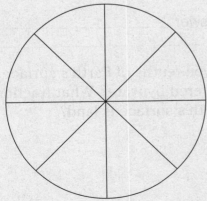

4. In the United States, $\frac{7}{10}$ of the population has brown hair, $\frac{3}{20}$ has blonde hair, $\frac{1}{10}$ has black hair, and $\frac{1}{20}$ are redheads. Make a circle graph to show the hair color of an average group of 20 people in the United States.

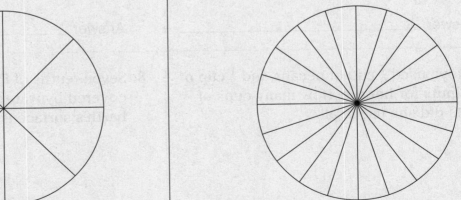

Problem-Solving Applications

Solve.

1. Isaac spent three-fourths of an hour practicing the violin. How many minutes did he practice? (1 hour = 60 minutes)

   Answer _____

2. Jan lives $\frac{3}{4}$ mile west of the library. Alice lives $\frac{1}{8}$ mile west of Jan. How far from the library does Alice live?

   Answer _____

3. Joe is $\frac{3}{4}$ inch taller than Tom. Tom is $\frac{1}{2}$ inch taller than Jack. How much taller is Joe than Jack?

   Answer _____

4. Bill walked $\frac{3}{8}$ mile in the morning and $\frac{1}{4}$ mile in the evening. How far did he walk altogether?

   Answer _____

5. Oak trees are very slow growers. They only grow $\frac{2}{5}$ inch a week. How many inches will an oak tree grow in 2 weeks?

   Answer _____

6. Joyce made bread and muffins. She used $\frac{3}{4}$ cup of flour for the bread and $\frac{5}{8}$ cup of flour for the muffins. How much flour did she use in all?

   Answer _____

7. Latoya used $\frac{7}{9}$ cup of pecans and $\frac{1}{2}$ cup of walnuts for her pie. How many cups of nuts did she use in all?

   Answer _____

8. Seven-tenths of Earth's surface is covered by water. What fraction of Earth's surface is land?

   Answer _____

Adding Mixed Numbers, Whole Numbers, and Fractions

To add mixed numbers, whole numbers, and fractions, first check for unlike denominators. Write mixed numbers and fractions as equivalent fractions with like denominators. Add the fractions. Then add the whole numbers and simplify.

Find: $2\frac{7}{12} + \frac{1}{4}$

Write the fractions with like denominators.	Add the fractions.	Add the whole numbers.	Simplify.
$2\frac{7}{12} = 2\frac{7}{12}$ $+ \ \frac{1}{4} = \ \frac{3}{12}$	$2\frac{7}{12} = 2\frac{7}{12}$ $+ \ \frac{1}{4} = \ \frac{3}{12}$ $\frac{10}{12}$	$2\frac{7}{12} = 2\frac{7}{12}$ $+ \ \frac{1}{4} = \ \frac{3}{12}$ $2\frac{10}{12}$	$2\frac{10}{12} = 2\frac{5}{6}$

Remember, $\frac{1}{4} = \frac{3}{12}$.
They are equivalent fractions.

PRACTICE

Add. Simplify.

	a	b	c	d
1.	$4\frac{1}{2} = 4\frac{2}{4}$ $+ \ \ \frac{1}{4} = \ \frac{1}{4}$ $4\frac{3}{4}$	$\frac{1}{2}$ $+ 8\frac{1}{8}$	$6\frac{1}{4}$ $+ \ \ \frac{1}{8}$	$\frac{1}{2}$ $+ 9\frac{3}{8}$
2.	$1 \ 2\frac{1}{3} = 12\frac{2}{6}$ $+ \ \ 9\frac{1}{6} = 9\frac{1}{6}$ $21\frac{3}{6} = 21\frac{1}{2}$	$8\frac{1}{2}$ $+ 9\frac{1}{10}$	$1 \ 2\frac{1}{5}$ $+ \ \ 7\frac{1}{10}$	$6\frac{1}{3}$ $+ 8\frac{1}{9}$
3.	$\frac{1}{3}$ $+ 2\frac{1}{4}$	$3\frac{1}{4}$ $+ \ \ \frac{2}{3}$	$7\frac{1}{2}$ $+ \ \ \frac{1}{3}$	$\frac{3}{8}$ $+ 1\frac{1}{7}$
4.	$5\frac{1}{8}$ $+ 6\frac{1}{6}$	$8\frac{1}{4}$ $+ 9\frac{1}{3}$	$4\frac{2}{5}$ $+ 7\frac{1}{2}$	$7\frac{1}{2}$ $+ 8\frac{3}{10}$

Adding Mixed Numbers with Large Sums

When adding mixed numbers, whole numbers, and fractions, your sum might contain an improper fraction. To regroup a sum that contains an improper fraction, first write the improper fraction as a mixed number. Then add and simplify.

Find: $5\frac{1}{3} + \frac{5}{7}$

Write the fractions with like denominators. Add.	The sum $5\frac{22}{21}$ contains an improper fraction. To regroup, write the improper fraction as a mixed number.	Then add.
$5\frac{1}{3} = 5\frac{7}{21}$ $+\ \frac{5}{7} = \ \frac{15}{21}$ $\overline{\qquad 5\frac{22}{21}}$	$\frac{22}{21} = 1\frac{1}{21}$	$5\frac{22}{21} = 5 + 1\frac{1}{21} = 6\frac{1}{21}$

PRACTICE

Add. Simplify.

       a   b   c   d

1. $4\frac{1}{2} = 4\frac{3}{6}$ $9\frac{2}{5}$ $3\frac{2}{3}$ $\frac{3}{7}$

     $+\ \ \frac{5}{6} = \ \frac{5}{6}$ $+\ \ \frac{5}{6}$ $+\ \ \frac{8}{9}$ $+\ 6\frac{7}{8}$

                 $4\frac{8}{6} = 5\frac{1}{3}$

2. $2\frac{3}{4}$ $9\frac{1}{3}$ $10\frac{5}{7}$ $1\frac{1}{2}$

     $+\ 7\frac{5}{6}$ $+\ 4\frac{7}{9}$ $+\ \ 7\frac{9}{11}$ $+\ 9\frac{11}{12}$

3. $9\frac{2}{3}$ $7\frac{3}{9}$ $10\frac{9}{10}$ $8\frac{1}{2}$

     $+\ \ \frac{3}{4}$ $+\ \ \frac{1}{2}$ $+\ \ \frac{2}{5}$ $+\ \ \frac{2}{3}$

4. $\frac{1}{3}$ $2\frac{3}{10}$ $1\frac{1}{2}$ $2\frac{3}{8}$

     $3\frac{2}{3}$ $15\frac{3}{5}$ $17\frac{1}{2}$ $\frac{5}{8}$

     $+\ 9\frac{7}{12}$ $+\ \ \frac{7}{10}$ $+\ \ \frac{7}{10}$ $+\ 7\frac{1}{2}$

PRACTICE

Add. Simplify.

	a	*b*	*c*	*d*
1.	$5\frac{5}{6}$ $+\ 4\frac{2}{6}$	$\frac{2}{3}$ $+\ 2\frac{5}{6}$	$9\frac{2}{5}$ $+\ \ \ \frac{5}{6}$	$15\frac{3}{4}$ $+\ \ \ \ \frac{1}{8}$
2.	$4\frac{3}{5}$ $+\ 1\frac{3}{5}$	$4\frac{4}{5}$ $+\ 2\frac{2}{3}$	$2\frac{3}{4}$ $+\ 8\frac{2}{3}$	$1\frac{6}{7}$ $+\ 6\frac{1}{3}$
3.	$\frac{1}{2}$ $+\ 5\frac{7}{9}$	$\frac{4}{5}$ $+\ 18\frac{2}{5}$	$9\frac{5}{6}$ $+\ \ \ \frac{9}{12}$	$3\frac{2}{9}$ $+\ 2\frac{2}{3}$
4.	$\frac{1}{4}$ $5\frac{1}{2}$ $+\ 4\frac{1}{4}$	$20\frac{3}{5}$ $4\frac{1}{5}$ $+\ \ \ \ \frac{3}{10}$	$15\frac{1}{2}$ $1\frac{3}{4}$ $+\ \ \ \ \frac{5}{6}$	$10\frac{1}{8}$ $\frac{5}{8}$ $+\ 10\frac{3}{4}$

Set up the problems. Then find the sums. Simplify.

       a   *b*   *c*

5. $\frac{3}{5}+5\frac{2}{10}=$ _____ $4\frac{5}{8}+\frac{1}{3}=$ _____ $10\frac{1}{3}+6\frac{1}{6}=$ _____

MIXED PRACTICE

Compare. Write <, >, or =.

	a	*b*	*c*
1.	838 _____ 833	57,215 _____ 57,215	1,642,085 _____ 1,462,085

Write in order from least to greatest.

2. 755   575   757   _____

3. 3,608   3,680   3,860   _____

Subtraction of Fractions with Different Denominators

To subtract fractions with different denominators, first rewrite the fractions as equivalent fractions with like denominators. Then subtract and simplify the answer.

Find: $\frac{4}{5} - \frac{3}{4}$

Write equivalent fractions with like denominators. Use the LCD.

$$\frac{4}{5} = \frac{4 \times 4}{5 \times 4} = \frac{16}{20}$$
$$-\frac{3}{4} = \frac{3 \times 5}{4 \times 5} = \frac{15}{20}$$

Subtract the numerators. Use the same denominators.

$$\frac{4}{5} = \frac{16}{20}$$
$$-\frac{3}{4} = \frac{15}{20}$$
$$\frac{1}{20}$$

GUIDED PRACTICE

Subtract. Simplify.

	a	b	c	d
1.	$\frac{1}{3} = \frac{4}{12}$ $-\frac{1}{4} = \frac{3}{12}$ $\frac{1}{12}$	$\frac{1}{4} = \frac{}{20}$ $-\frac{1}{5} = \frac{}{20}$	$\frac{3}{5} = \frac{}{10}$ $-\frac{1}{2} = \frac{}{10}$	$\frac{2}{3} = \frac{}{6}$ $-\frac{1}{2} = \frac{}{6}$
2.	$\frac{1}{2} = \frac{}{12}$ $-\frac{1}{12} = \frac{}{12}$	$\frac{5}{6} = \frac{}{6}$ $-\frac{1}{2} = \frac{}{6}$	$\frac{1}{3} = \frac{}{6}$ $-\frac{1}{6} = \frac{}{6}$	$\frac{5}{6} = \frac{}{6}$ $-\frac{1}{3} = \frac{}{6}$
3.	$\frac{1}{2} = \frac{}{8}$ $-\frac{1}{8} = \frac{}{8}$	$\frac{3}{4} = \frac{}{8}$ $-\frac{1}{8} = \frac{}{8}$	$\frac{3}{7} = \frac{}{35}$ $-\frac{1}{5} = \frac{}{35}$	$\frac{7}{10} = \frac{}{10}$ $-\frac{1}{2} = \frac{}{10}$
4.	$\frac{7}{8} = \frac{}{40}$ $-\frac{3}{10} = \frac{}{40}$	$\frac{2}{3} = \frac{}{6}$ $-\frac{1}{6} = \frac{}{6}$	$\frac{4}{5} = \frac{}{15}$ $-\frac{2}{3} = \frac{}{15}$	$\frac{5}{7} = \frac{}{21}$ $-\frac{1}{3} = \frac{}{21}$

PRACTICE

Subtract. Simplify.

	a	b	c	d
1.	$\frac{7}{8} = \frac{7}{8}$	$\frac{11}{12}$	$\frac{9}{11}$	$\frac{5}{7}$
	$-\frac{1}{4} = \frac{2}{8}$	$-\frac{1}{3}$	$-\frac{3}{5}$	$-\frac{1}{2}$
	$\frac{5}{8}$			
2.	$\frac{5}{6} = \frac{10}{12}$	$\frac{5}{6}$	$\frac{4}{5}$	$\frac{1}{2}$
	$-\frac{1}{4} = \frac{3}{12}$	$-\frac{3}{8}$	$-\frac{1}{2}$	$-\frac{1}{5}$
	$\frac{7}{12}$			
3.	$\frac{4}{5} = \frac{8}{10}$	$\frac{5}{6}$	$\frac{3}{4}$	$\frac{7}{9}$
	$-\frac{3}{10} = \frac{3}{10}$	$-\frac{5}{9}$	$-\frac{3}{8}$	$-\frac{1}{4}$
	$\frac{5}{10} = \frac{1}{2}$			

Set up the problems. Then find the differences. Simplify.

        a   b   c

4. $\frac{14}{15} - \frac{1}{3} =$ _____ $\frac{8}{9} - \frac{3}{8} =$ _____ $\frac{11}{12} - \frac{3}{8} =$ _____

$\frac{14}{15}$
$-\frac{1}{3}$

MIXED PRACTICE

Find each answer.

	a	b	c	d
1.	$3,429$	$2,569$	246	$1,493$
	$+2,176$	$+8,754$	-129	$-\ \ \ 647$
2.	219	204	$17\overline{)527}$	$31\overline{)403}$
	$\times\ \ 27$	$\times\ \ 23$		

Subtraction of Fractions and Mixed Numbers from Whole Numbers

Sometimes you will need to subtract a fraction from a whole number. Write the whole number as a mixed number with a like denominator. Subtract the fractions. Subtract the whole numbers.

Find: $7 - 2\frac{5}{8}$

To subtract, you need two fractions with like denominators.	Write 7 as a mixed number with 8 as the denominator.	Subtract the fractions.	Subtract the whole numbers.
$\begin{array}{r} 7 \\ -2\frac{5}{8} \\ \hline \end{array}$	$7 = 6 + \frac{8}{8} = 6\frac{8}{8}$ **Remember,** $\frac{8}{8} = 1$	$\begin{array}{r} 7 = 6\frac{8}{8} \\ -2\frac{5}{8} = 2\frac{5}{8} \\ \hline \frac{3}{8} \end{array}$	$\begin{array}{r} 7 = 6\frac{8}{8} \\ -2\frac{5}{8} = 2\frac{5}{8} \\ \hline 4\frac{3}{8} \end{array}$

Write each whole number as a mixed number.

	a	b	c	d
1.	$8 = 7 + \frac{4}{4} = 7\frac{4}{4}$	$12 = 11 + \frac{3}{} =$	$9 = 8 + \frac{}{6} =$	$4 = 3 + \frac{5}{} =$
2.	$15 = 14 + \frac{}{7} =$	$20 = 19 + \frac{2}{} =$	$18 = 17 + \frac{}{8} =$	$28 = 27 + \frac{12}{} =$

Subtract. Simplify.

	a	b	c	d
3.	$\begin{array}{r} 8 = 7\frac{3}{3} \\ -4\frac{2}{3} = 4\frac{2}{3} \\ \hline 3\frac{1}{3} \end{array}$	$\begin{array}{r} 4 = 3\frac{}{4} \\ -2\frac{3}{4} = 2\frac{3}{4} \\ \hline \end{array}$	$\begin{array}{r} 6 = 5\frac{}{8} \\ -2\frac{5}{8} = 2\frac{5}{8} \\ \hline \end{array}$	$\begin{array}{r} 1\,4 = 1\,3\frac{}{6} \\ -9\frac{5}{6} = 9\frac{5}{6} \\ \hline \end{array}$
4.	$\begin{array}{r} 7 = 6\frac{6}{6} \\ -2\frac{5}{6} = 2\frac{5}{6} \\ \hline 4\frac{1}{6} \end{array}$	$\begin{array}{r} 8 = \\ -4\frac{3}{4} = \\ \hline \end{array}$	$\begin{array}{r} 7 = \\ -3\frac{3}{7} = \\ \hline \end{array}$	$\begin{array}{r} 1\,4 = \\ -6\frac{2}{3} = \\ \hline \end{array}$
5.	$\begin{array}{r} 4 = 3\frac{2}{2} \\ -\frac{1}{2} = \frac{1}{2} \\ \hline 3\frac{1}{2} \end{array}$	$\begin{array}{r} 5 = \\ -\frac{1}{3} = \\ \hline \end{array}$	$\begin{array}{r} 9 = \\ -\frac{2}{5} = \\ \hline \end{array}$	$\begin{array}{r} 1\,2 = \\ -\frac{5}{9} = \\ \hline \end{array}$

PRACTICE

Subtract. Simplify.

	a	b	c	d
1.	15 $-\ 12\frac{1}{2}$	19 $-\ 14\frac{5}{8}$	27 $-\ 13\frac{5}{7}$	29 $-\ 6\frac{1}{9}$
2.	8 $-\ \frac{1}{5}$	7 $-\ \frac{2}{7}$	12 $-\ 8\frac{1}{5}$	15 $-\ \frac{3}{10}$
3.	12 $-\ 9\frac{1}{6}$	16 $-\ \frac{3}{4}$	13 $-\ 10\frac{5}{9}$	9 $-\ \frac{3}{5}$
4.	6 $-\ 4\frac{3}{8}$	8 $-\ 4\frac{1}{4}$	15 $-\ 4\frac{7}{12}$	19 $-\ 7\frac{5}{6}$

Set up the problems. Then find the differences. Simplify.

	a	b	c
5.	$15 - 12\frac{2}{5} = $ _____ 15 $-12\frac{2}{5}$	$7 - 3\frac{4}{9} = $ _____	$13 - \frac{1}{3} = $ _____
6.	$14 - 8\frac{7}{10} = $ _____	$6 - \frac{9}{16} = $ _____	$19 - 4\frac{5}{6} = $ _____

Estimate each sum or difference.

	a	b	c	d
1.	$5,089 \rightarrow$ $+2,306 \rightarrow$	$2,053 \rightarrow$ $+2,276 \rightarrow$	$6,314 \rightarrow$ $-2,585 \rightarrow$	$4,020 \rightarrow$ $-1,492 \rightarrow$

Subtraction of Mixed Numbers with Regrouping

To subtract mixed numbers, it may be necessary to regroup first. Write the whole number part as a mixed number. Add the mixed number and the fraction. Then subtract and simplify.

Find: $8\frac{7}{12} - 2\frac{3}{4}$

Write the fractions with like denominators. Compare the numerators. $$8\frac{7}{12} = 8\frac{7}{12}$$ $$-2\frac{3}{4} = 2\frac{9}{12}$$	$\frac{9}{12}$ is greater than $\frac{7}{12}$. You can't subtract the fractions. To regroup, write **8** as a mixed number. $$8 = 7\frac{12}{12}$$	Add the mixed number and the fraction. $$8\frac{7}{12} = 7\frac{12}{12} + \frac{7}{12} = 7\frac{19}{12}$$ Remember, $\frac{19}{12}$ is an improper fraction.	Now you can subtract and simplify. $$8\frac{7}{12} = 7\frac{19}{12}$$ $$-2\frac{9}{12} = 2\frac{9}{12}$$ $$5\frac{10}{12} = 5\frac{5}{6}$$

GUIDED PRACTICE

Regroup each mixed number.

        a   *b*   *c*

1. $5\frac{2}{7} = 4\frac{7}{7} + \frac{2}{7} = 4\frac{9}{7}$ $8\frac{5}{12} =$ $5\frac{1}{3} =$

2. $4\frac{6}{9} =$ $6\frac{7}{10} =$ $12\frac{3}{5} =$

Subtract. Simplify.

        a   *b*   *c*

3.

$$8\frac{1}{5} = 7\frac{6}{5}$$
$$-2\frac{4}{5} = 2\frac{4}{5}$$
$$\overline{5\frac{2}{5}}$$

$$7\frac{1}{4} = 6\frac{}{4}$$
$$-\frac{3}{4} = \frac{3}{4}$$

$$8\frac{7}{12} = 7\frac{}{12}$$
$$-4\frac{11}{12} = 4\frac{11}{12}$$

4.

$$9\frac{1}{8} = 9\frac{1}{8} = 8\frac{9}{8}$$
$$-\frac{3}{4} = \frac{6}{8} = \frac{6}{8}$$
$$\overline{8\frac{3}{8}}$$

$$12\frac{1}{5} = 12\frac{2}{10} =$$
$$-6\frac{3}{10} = 6\frac{3}{10} =$$

$$14\frac{2}{9} = 14\frac{2}{9} =$$
$$-8\frac{2}{3} = 8\frac{6}{9} =$$

5.

$$5\frac{1}{3} = 5\frac{4}{12} = 4\frac{16}{12}$$
$$-2\frac{3}{4} = 2\frac{9}{12} = 2\frac{9}{12}$$
$$\overline{2\frac{7}{12}}$$

$$9\frac{1}{8} = 9\frac{5}{40} =$$
$$-6\frac{3}{5} = 6\frac{24}{40} =$$

$$17\frac{1}{12} = 17\frac{3}{36} =$$
$$-\frac{7}{9} = \frac{28}{36} =$$

PRACTICE

Subtract. Simplify.

	a	b	c
1.	$9\frac{3}{8}$ $-\ \ \frac{1}{2}$	$10\frac{1}{3}$ $-\ 8\frac{2}{3}$	$7\frac{1}{5}$ $-\ 4\frac{5}{8}$
2.	$15\frac{1}{6}$ $-\ 12\frac{1}{4}$	$25\frac{1}{8}$ $-\ 12\frac{1}{4}$	$19\frac{1}{9}$ $-\ \ \frac{7}{8}$
3.	$16\frac{1}{12}$ $-\ \ 9\frac{11}{12}$	$12\frac{1}{10}$ $-\ \ \ \frac{1}{5}$	$16\frac{1}{2}$ $-\ \ 8\frac{4}{9}$

Set up the problems. Then find the differences. Simplify.

         a   b   c

4. $6\frac{3}{5} - 4\frac{9}{10} =$ _____ $9\frac{1}{4} - 7\frac{3}{7} =$ _____ $15\frac{1}{3} - \frac{2}{3} =$ _____

$6\frac{3}{5}$
$-4\frac{9}{10}$

5. $12\frac{1}{8} - \frac{3}{4} =$ _____ $8\frac{1}{8} - 3\frac{5}{8} =$ _____ $16\frac{2}{5} - 4\frac{1}{2} =$ _____

MIXED PRACTICE

Multiply or divide.

	a	b	c	d
1.	$\begin{array}{r}404\\ \times\ \ 28\end{array}$	$5\,6\overline{)1\,3,6\,0\,8}$	$\begin{array}{r}751\\ \times\ \ 88\end{array}$	$7\,3\overline{)4\,6,7\,2\,0}$

Problem-Solving Strategy: Use Estimation

Stacey's bowl holds 15 cups of punch. Her recipe for punch is $9\frac{1}{3}$ cups of juice mixed with $6\frac{3}{4}$ cups of ginger ale. Does she need a bigger bowl?

Understand the problem.

- **What do you want to know?**
  if the punch will fit in the bowl

- **What information is given?**
  The bowl holds 15 cups.
  The punch is made with $9\frac{1}{3}$ cups of juice and $6\frac{3}{4}$ cups of ginger ale.

Plan how to solve it.

- **What strategy can you use?**
  Since the problem is not asking for an exact answer, you can use estimation to find the sum of the punch ingredients.

Solve it.

- **How can you use this strategy to solve the problem?**
  Round the mixed numbers to whole numbers. If the fractional part is less than $\frac{1}{2}$, drop the fraction and leave the whole number unchanged. If it is greater than or equal to $\frac{1}{2}$, round up to the next whole number.

$$
\begin{array}{llll}
9\frac{1}{3} & \text{Think: } \frac{1}{3} < \frac{1}{2} \text{ Round down.} & \rightarrow & 9 \\
+ 6\frac{3}{4} & \text{Think: } \frac{3}{4} > \frac{1}{2} \text{ Round up.} & \rightarrow & + 7 \\
\hline
& & & \text{16 cups of punch}
\end{array}
$$

- **What is the answer?**
  Stacey needs a bigger bowl.

Look back and check your answer.

- **Is your answer reasonable?**
  You can check your estimate by finding the exact answer.

$$
\begin{array}{rl}
9\frac{1}{3} = & 9\frac{4}{12} \\
+ 6\frac{3}{4} = & 6\frac{9}{12} \\
\hline
15\frac{13}{12} = & 16\frac{1}{12}
\end{array}
$$

The exact answer shows that the 15-cup bowl is not large enough to hold all the punch.
The estimate is reasonable.

Use estimation to solve each problem.

1. Ellen has 4 cups of sugar. She needs $3\frac{2}{3}$ cups to make a cake and $1\frac{1}{4}$ cups to make the icing. Does she have enough sugar?

Answer _____

2. Tyrone had $12\frac{4}{5}$ yards of material. He used $8\frac{1}{6}$ yards to make curtains. He needs 2 yards to make a pillow. Does he have enough material?

Answer _____

3. Maya hiked $15\frac{3}{8}$ miles on Saturday and $13\frac{1}{2}$ miles on Sunday. Her 2-day goal was to hike 30 miles. Did she reach her goal?

Answer _____

4. Tom planned to sell his stock when it reached $25 per share. In the morning, the stock was $19\frac{1}{5}$ per share. It went up $6\frac{2}{9}$ by the afternoon. Did he sell his stock?

Answer _____

5. Kim leaves her house at 10:00 A.M. It takes $1\frac{1}{2}$ hours to drive to the airport and $\frac{3}{4}$ hour to check in. Will she make her 12:00 P.M. flight?

Answer _____

6. It snowed $2\frac{1}{4}$ inches on Monday, 3 inches on Tuesday, and $\frac{5}{8}$ inch on Wednesday. About how many inches did it snow in the three days altogether?

Answer _____

Problem-Solving Applications

Solve. Simplify.

1. When Kelly was born, she weighed $7\frac{1}{2}$ pounds. By her first check-up, she had gained $2\frac{2}{3}$ pounds. How much did Kelly weigh at her first check-up?

   Answer _____

2. Trey worked $8\frac{1}{5}$ hours on Friday, 10 hours on Saturday, and only $\frac{1}{2}$ hour on Sunday. How many hours did he work altogether?

   Answer _____

3. Maria bought $\frac{1}{2}$ pound of modeling clay. She used $\frac{3}{8}$ pound to make an ornament. How much did she have left?

   Answer _____

4. Elliot lives $5\frac{3}{4}$ miles from school. Mei lives $2\frac{1}{6}$ miles from school. How much farther from school does Elliot live than Mei?

   Answer _____

5. In January, it rained $3\frac{3}{4}$ inches. It rained $4\frac{1}{5}$ inches in February. How much more did it rain in February than in January?

   Answer _____

6. Taneeka had 2 yards of speaker wire. She used $\frac{7}{8}$ yard to set up her stereo. How much wire did she have left?

   Answer _____

7. It takes 50 gallons of maple sap to make 1 gallon of syrup. Don collects $29\frac{2}{3}$ gallons of sap. How much more sap does he need to make 1 gallon of syrup?

   Answer _____

8. The two fish Matthew caught yesterday weighed $7\frac{3}{4}$ pounds in all. One of the fish weighed $3\frac{1}{2}$ pounds. How much did the other fish weigh?

   Answer _____

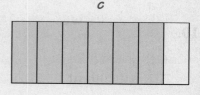

Write the fraction and the word name for the part that is shaded.

        a   *b*   *c*

1.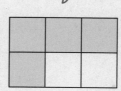

_____ or _____   _____ or _____   _____ or _____

Write as a whole or mixed number. Simplify.

        a   *b*   *c*   *d*

2. $\frac{35}{5} =$ _____ $\frac{26}{3} =$ _____ $\frac{15}{3} =$ _____ $\frac{21}{6} =$ _____

Write as an improper fraction.

        a   *b*   *c*   *d*

3. $3\frac{1}{4} =$ _____ $2\frac{7}{8} =$ _____ $4\frac{3}{5} =$ _____ $1\frac{7}{10} =$ _____

Rewrite each fraction as an equivalent fraction in higher terms.

        a   *b*   *c*   *d*

4. $\frac{4}{7} = \frac{}{21}$ $\frac{1}{9} = \frac{}{45}$ $\frac{2}{3} = \frac{}{24}$ $\frac{5}{6} = \frac{}{18}$

5. $\frac{2}{7} = \frac{}{14}$ $\frac{3}{8} = \frac{}{16}$ $\frac{4}{5} = \frac{}{15}$ $\frac{1}{4} = \frac{}{20}$

Use the LCD to write equivalent fractions.

        a   *b*   *c*   *d*

6. $\frac{1}{4} =$ $\frac{1}{5} =$ $\frac{3}{8} =$ $\frac{1}{2} =$

     $\frac{1}{3} =$ $\frac{3}{4} =$ $\frac{2}{3} =$ $\frac{4}{11} =$

7. $\frac{2}{5} =$ $\frac{3}{7} =$ $\frac{4}{9} =$ $\frac{6}{7} =$

     $\frac{2}{3} =$ $\frac{1}{2} =$ $\frac{1}{4} =$ $\frac{5}{11} =$

Simplify.

        a   *b*   *c*   *d*

8. $\frac{4}{24} =$ $\frac{3}{9} =$ $\frac{2}{30} =$ $\frac{15}{45} =$

9. $\frac{6}{42} =$ $\frac{12}{20} =$ $\frac{3}{27} =$ $\frac{16}{32} =$

UNIT 2 Review

Add. Simplify.

	a	b	c	d
10.	$\frac{2}{7}$ $+ \frac{6}{7}$	$\frac{2}{3}$ $+ \frac{1}{9}$	1 $+ 2\frac{3}{11}$	$3\frac{3}{8}$ $+ 2\frac{1}{5}$

11. $3\frac{8}{9}$ $+ 5$ $2\frac{5}{12}$ $+ 4\frac{7}{8}$ $1\frac{9}{10}$ $+ 3\frac{4}{5}$ $\frac{1}{6}$ $+ \frac{2}{7}$

12. $\frac{3}{4}$ $+ \frac{5}{6}$ $\frac{4}{7}$ $+ 15\frac{1}{3}$ $\frac{6}{11}$ $+ 5\frac{9}{11}$ 4 $+ \frac{9}{16}$

13. $1\frac{5}{6}$ $\frac{2}{3}$ $+ 4$ $9\frac{2}{3}$ $\frac{1}{9}$ $+ 12$ $\frac{5}{6}$ $9\frac{1}{4}$ $+ 18$ $6\frac{7}{8}$ $3\frac{4}{5}$ $+ 2$

Subtract. Simplify.

	a	b	c	d
14.	$\frac{5}{8}$ $- \frac{1}{3}$	8 $- 2\frac{2}{5}$	3 $- \frac{3}{7}$	$5\frac{11}{12}$ $- 3\frac{1}{6}$

15. 4 $- 3\frac{1}{2}$ 2 $- \frac{11}{12}$ $\frac{5}{8}$ $- \frac{3}{8}$ $\frac{5}{6}$ $- \frac{1}{4}$

16. $7\frac{1}{4}$ $- 2\frac{5}{9}$ $\frac{4}{5}$ $- \frac{1}{2}$ $9\frac{1}{12}$ $- 2\frac{5}{8}$ $2\frac{1}{4}$ $- \frac{3}{4}$

17. $10\frac{3}{5}$ $- 8\frac{1}{4}$ $4\frac{1}{7}$ $- \frac{2}{7}$ $5\frac{6}{9}$ $- 1\frac{4}{5}$ $\frac{7}{11}$ $- \frac{5}{9}$

Make a graph to solve each problem.

18. The 10 members of the book club voted for their favorite kind of book. Biographies got $\frac{2}{5}$ of the votes, fiction got $\frac{1}{2}$, and cookbooks got $\frac{1}{10}$. Make a circle graph to show the results of the vote.

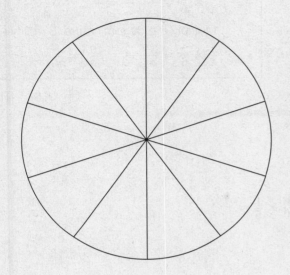

19. On an average day, Tim sleeps $\frac{1}{3}$ of the hours, works $\frac{1}{3}$ of the hours, and exercises for 1 hour. The rest of the day is free time. Make a circle graph to show how Tim spends an average day. (1 day = 24 hours)

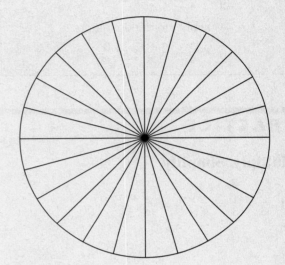

Use estimation to solve each problem.

20. Sara has 5 pounds of potting soil. She needs $2\frac{1}{5}$ pounds for her herb garden and $3\frac{1}{2}$ pounds for her flowers. Does she have enough soil?

21. Ted bought $10\frac{1}{4}$ feet of wood. He used $6\frac{2}{3}$ feet to build book shelves. He needs 2 feet to make a frame. Does he have enough wood?

Answer _____

Answer _____

Multiplication of Fractions

To multiply fractions, multiply the numerators and multiply the denominators. Simplify the product.

Find: $\frac{1}{2} \times \frac{3}{4}$

> Multiply the numerators.
>
> $\frac{1}{2} \times \frac{3}{4} = \frac{1 \times 3}{} = \frac{3}{}$
>
> Multiply the denominators.
>
> $\frac{1}{2} \times \frac{3}{4} = \frac{1 \times 3}{2 \times 4} = \frac{3}{8}$

Find: $\frac{3}{4} \times \frac{2}{6}$

> Multiply the numerators.
>
> $\frac{3}{4} \times \frac{2}{6} = \frac{3 \times 2}{} = \frac{6}{}$
>
> Multiply the denominators. Simplify.
>
> $\frac{3}{4} \times \frac{2}{6} = \frac{3 \times 2}{4 \times 6} = \frac{6}{24} = \frac{1}{4}$

PRACTICE

Multiply. Simplify.

      a   *b*

1. $\frac{2}{5} \times \frac{1}{3} = \frac{2 \times 1}{5 \times 3} = \frac{2}{15}$ $\frac{3}{10} \times \frac{1}{5} =$

2. $\frac{4}{7} \times \frac{3}{5} =$ $\frac{5}{6} \times \frac{7}{8} =$

3. $\frac{1}{2} \times \frac{4}{7} =$ $\frac{1}{3} \times \frac{6}{11} =$

4. $\frac{3}{4} \times \frac{1}{3} =$ $\frac{5}{8} \times \frac{3}{10} =$

5. $\frac{4}{10} \times \frac{5}{16} =$ $\frac{3}{12} \times \frac{1}{3} =$

6. $\frac{4}{9} \times \frac{3}{8} =$ $\frac{5}{6} \times \frac{3}{10} =$

Multiplication of Fractions Using Cancellation

Instead of simplifying fractions after they have been multiplied, it may be possible to use **cancellation** before multiplying. To cancel, find a common factor of a numerator and a denominator. Divide the numerator and the denominator by the common factor. Then multiply, using the new numerator and denominator.

Find: $\frac{3}{4} \times \frac{2}{5}$ **using cancellation.**

Find the common factor.	Cancel.	Multiply the new numerators and denominators. Simplify.
$\frac{3}{4} \times \frac{2}{5}$	$\frac{3}{\overset{}{\underset{2}{4}}} \times \frac{\overset{1}{2}}{5}$	$\frac{3 \times 1}{2 \times 5} = \frac{3}{10}$
The common factor of 4 and 2 is 2.	Divide both the 4 and the 2 by 2.	

PRACTICE

Multiply using cancellation.

           a   *b*

1. $\frac{3}{4} \times \frac{1}{3} = \frac{\overset{1}{\cancel{3}}}{4} \times \frac{1}{\underset{1}{\cancel{3}}} = \frac{1 \times 1}{4 \times 1} = \frac{1}{4}$ $\frac{7}{8} \times \frac{4}{9} =$

2. $\frac{4}{7} \times \frac{3}{8} =$ $\frac{5}{16} \times \frac{1}{5} =$

3. $\frac{2}{3} \times \frac{1}{8} =$ $\frac{3}{4} \times \frac{1}{9} =$

4. $\frac{7}{10} \times \frac{5}{6} =$ $\frac{3}{4} \times \frac{13}{15} =$

5. $\frac{5}{6} \times \frac{3}{10} =$ $\frac{4}{9} \times \frac{3}{8} =$

6. $\frac{2}{3} \times \frac{3}{4} =$ $\frac{4}{5} \times \frac{5}{8} =$

Multiplication of Whole Numbers by Fractions

To multiply a whole number by a fraction, first write the whole number as an improper fraction. Use cancellation if possible. Multiply the numerators and the denominators. Simplify.

Find: $8 \times \frac{5}{16}$

Write the whole number as an improper fraction.	Cancel.	Multiply using the new numbers. Simplify.
$8 \times \frac{5}{16} = \frac{8}{1} \times \frac{5}{16}$	$\overset{1}{\cancel{8}} \times \frac{5}{\underset{2}{\cancel{16}}}$ Divide 8 and 16 by 8.	$\frac{1 \times 5}{1 \times 2} = \frac{5}{2} = 2\frac{1}{2}$

GUIDED PRACTICE

Write each whole number as a fraction.

	a	b	c	d	e	f
1.	$7 = \frac{7}{1}$	$18 =$	$20 =$	$4 =$	$12 =$	$15 =$

Multiply using cancellation. Simplify.

	a	b	c
2.	$10 \times \frac{1}{5} = \frac{\overset{2}{\cancel{10}}}{1} \times \frac{1}{\underset{1}{\cancel{5}}} = \frac{2 \times 1}{1 \times 1} = 2$	$14 \times \frac{2}{7} =$	$15 \times \frac{3}{10} =$
3.	$9 \times \frac{1}{6} =$	$12 \times \frac{3}{4} =$	$8 \times \frac{5}{6} =$
4.	$\frac{2}{3} \times 9 =$	$\frac{3}{10} \times 25 =$	$\frac{4}{5} \times 25 =$
5.	$\frac{8}{9} \times 27 =$	$\frac{11}{16} \times 24 =$	$\frac{5}{8} \times 32 =$
6.	$\frac{7}{16} \times 8 =$	$32 \times \frac{5}{8} =$	$\frac{7}{9} \times 36 =$

PRACTICE

Multiply using cancellation. Simplify.

	a	b	c
1.	$25 \times \frac{3}{5} =$	$30 \times \frac{3}{10} =$	$16 \times \frac{7}{8} =$
2.	$\frac{6}{11} \times 33 =$	$\frac{4}{15} \times 42 =$	$\frac{3}{4} \times 28 =$
3.	$\frac{13}{20} \times 35 =$	$\frac{3}{7} \times 35 =$	$\frac{8}{9} \times 45 =$
4.	$48 \times \frac{5}{16} =$	$18 \times \frac{4}{9} =$	$27 \times \frac{2}{3} =$
5.	$\frac{6}{7} \times 21 =$	$\frac{4}{9} \times 6 =$	$\frac{5}{8} \times 14 =$
6.	$\frac{5}{16} \times 8 =$	$\frac{5}{6} \times 12 =$	$16 \times \frac{7}{32} =$
7.	$\frac{5}{32} \times 8 =$	$44 \times \frac{3}{8} =$	$25 \times \frac{9}{10} =$

MIXED PRACTICE

Write as an improper fraction.

	a	b	c	d
1.	$3\frac{5}{8} =$	$4\frac{1}{5} =$	$9\frac{3}{5} =$	$3\frac{7}{10} =$

Write as a mixed number.

	a	b	c	d
2.	$\frac{16}{3} =$	$\frac{35}{8} =$	$\frac{12}{7} =$	$\frac{20}{6} =$

Multiplication of Mixed Numbers by Whole Numbers

To multiply a mixed number by a whole number, first write the mixed number and the whole number as improper fractions. Use cancellation if possible. Multiply the new numerators and denominators. Simplify the answer.

Find: $4\frac{1}{2} \times 6$

Write the whole number and the mixed number as improper fractions.	Cancel.	Multiply the new numerators and denominators. Simplify.
$4\frac{1}{2} \times 6 = \frac{9}{2} \times \frac{6}{1}$	$\frac{9}{2} \times \frac{\overset{3}{\cancel{6}}}{\underset{1}{1}}$	$\frac{9 \times 3}{1 \times 1} = \frac{27}{1} = 27$

PRACTICE

Multiply. Simplify. Use cancellation if possible.

	a	b	c
1.	$2\frac{1}{2} \times 6 =$	$2\frac{1}{3} \times 3 =$	$4\frac{1}{2} \times 8 =$
	$\frac{5}{2} \times \frac{\overset{3}{\cancel{6}}}{\underset{1}{1}} = \frac{15}{1} = 15$		
2.	$4 \times 2\frac{1}{2} =$	$6 \times 2\frac{1}{3} =$	$1\frac{3}{4} \times 8 =$
3.	$6 \times 2\frac{1}{6} =$	$9 \times 2\frac{1}{3} =$	$4 \times 12\frac{1}{2} =$
4.	$3\frac{1}{3} \times 20 =$	$2 \times 5\frac{3}{4} =$	$4 \times 3\frac{1}{5} =$
	$\frac{10}{3} \times \frac{20}{1} = \frac{200}{3} = 66\frac{2}{3}$		
5.	$4 \times 2\frac{1}{10} =$	$5 \times 2\frac{1}{15} =$	$11 \times 7\frac{4}{22} =$
6.	$8\frac{4}{15} \times 5 =$	$4\frac{1}{9} \times 30 =$	$2\frac{4}{9} \times 2 =$

Multiplication of Mixed Numbers by Fractions

To multiply a mixed number by a fraction, first write the mixed number as an improper fraction. Use cancellation if possible. Multiply the new numerators and denominators. Simplify.

Find: $2\frac{1}{4} \times \frac{1}{3}$

Write the mixed number as an improper fraction.	Cancel.	Multiply the new numerators and denominators.
$2\frac{1}{4} \times \frac{1}{3} = \frac{9}{4} \times \frac{1}{3}$	$\frac{\overset{3}{\cancel{9}}}{4} \times \frac{1}{\underset{1}{\cancel{3}}}$	$\frac{3 \times 1}{4 \times 1} = \frac{3}{4}$

PRACTICE

Multiply. Simplify. Use cancellation if possible.

	a	*b*	*c*
1.	$\frac{2}{5} \times 1\frac{1}{2} =$ $\frac{\overset{1}{\cancel{2}}}{5} \times \frac{3}{\underset{1}{\cancel{2}}} = \frac{3}{5}$	$\frac{3}{8} \times 1\frac{3}{5} =$	$\frac{1}{5} \times 4\frac{1}{6} =$
2.	$\frac{7}{8} \times 2\frac{2}{5} =$	$1\frac{1}{4} \times \frac{3}{5} =$	$\frac{7}{10} \times 1\frac{3}{14} =$
3.	$\frac{7}{10} \times 1\frac{1}{3} =$	$\frac{2}{3} \times 5\frac{7}{8} =$	$\frac{4}{5} \times 6\frac{3}{4} =$
4.	$2\frac{2}{3} \times \frac{3}{16} =$	$1\frac{1}{4} \times \frac{8}{15} =$	$2\frac{1}{4} \times \frac{4}{9} =$
5.	$4\frac{1}{2} \times \frac{2}{3} =$	$5\frac{1}{4} \times \frac{2}{3} =$	$8\frac{3}{4} \times \frac{2}{5} =$
6.	$12\frac{1}{2} \times \frac{4}{5} =$	$2\frac{3}{4} \times \frac{4}{22} =$	$3\frac{3}{4} \times \frac{16}{20} =$

Multiplication of Mixed Numbers by Mixed Numbers

To multiply a mixed number by a mixed number, write both mixed numbers as improper fractions. Use cancellation if possible. Then multiply the new numerators and denominators. Simplify.

Find: $3\frac{2}{3} \times 4\frac{1}{2}$

Write the mixed numbers as improper fractions.	Cancel.	Multiply the new numerators and denominators. Simplify.
$3\frac{2}{3} \times 4\frac{1}{2} = \frac{11}{3} \times \frac{9}{2}$	$\frac{11}{\cancel{3}_{1}} \times \frac{\cancel{9}^{3}}{2}$	$\frac{11 \times 3}{1 \times 2} = \frac{33}{2} = 16\frac{1}{2}$

GUIDED PRACTICE

Multiply. Simplify. Use cancellation if possible.

  a
  b
  c

1. $3\frac{1}{5} \times 2\frac{1}{4} =$ $\qquad$ $1\frac{1}{2} \times 1\frac{1}{2} =$ $\qquad$ $1\frac{2}{3} \times 1\frac{3}{5} =$

$\frac{\cancel{16}^{4}}{5} \times \frac{9}{\cancel{4}_{1}} = \frac{36}{5} = 7\frac{1}{5}$

2. $2\frac{1}{2} \times 3\frac{1}{3} =$ $\qquad$ $4\frac{1}{3} \times 3\frac{3}{4} =$ $\qquad$ $2\frac{3}{4} \times 2\frac{2}{3} =$

3. $5\frac{1}{4} \times 3\frac{1}{2} =$ $\qquad$ $4\frac{1}{2} \times 3\frac{1}{5} =$ $\qquad$ $6\frac{3}{4} \times 8\frac{1}{3} =$

4. $2\frac{1}{2} \times 3\frac{1}{2} =$ $\qquad$ $3\frac{3}{5} \times 2\frac{3}{4} =$ $\qquad$ $3\frac{3}{8} \times 5\frac{1}{3} =$

5. $4\frac{4}{5} \times 3\frac{1}{8} =$ $\qquad$ $4\frac{2}{7} \times 2\frac{1}{10} =$ $\qquad$ $5\frac{5}{8} \times 2\frac{2}{3} =$

6. $3\frac{3}{5} \times 3\frac{1}{3} =$ $\qquad$ $2\frac{4}{10} \times 3\frac{1}{3} =$ $\qquad$ $4\frac{4}{5} \times 1\frac{7}{8} =$

Multiply. Simplify. Use cancellation if possible.

	a	*b*	*c*
1.	$3\frac{3}{4} \times 1\frac{1}{3} =$	$4\frac{1}{2} \times 2\frac{4}{5} =$	$2\frac{2}{3} \times 5\frac{1}{5} =$
2.	$3\frac{1}{2} \times 3\frac{2}{5} =$	$1\frac{3}{4} \times 2\frac{1}{4} =$	$3\frac{1}{3} \times 4\frac{1}{3} =$
3.	$2\frac{1}{5} \times 6\frac{1}{4} =$	$7\frac{1}{3} \times 3\frac{1}{4} =$	$4\frac{1}{3} \times 5\frac{2}{5} =$
4.	$3\frac{1}{2} \times 8\frac{1}{6} =$	$6\frac{2}{3} \times 1\frac{1}{4} =$	$5\frac{1}{5} \times 8\frac{2}{5} =$
5.	$10\frac{1}{2} \times 1\frac{1}{2} =$	$6\frac{1}{6} \times 3\frac{1}{3} =$	$2\frac{3}{5} \times 2\frac{1}{4} =$
6.	$5\frac{5}{6} \times 3\frac{1}{4} =$	$4\frac{2}{3} \times 3\frac{3}{7} =$	$7\frac{1}{3} \times 1\frac{7}{9} =$
7.	$4\frac{1}{2} \times 4\frac{1}{7} =$	$1\frac{2}{3} \times 8\frac{3}{5} =$	$2\frac{1}{4} \times 5\frac{1}{3} =$

MIXED PRACTICE

Add or subtract. Simplify.

	a	*b*	*c*	*d*
1.	$\frac{4}{5}$ $-\frac{1}{3}$	$6\frac{1}{4}$ $+ 3\frac{2}{3}$	5 $-\frac{4}{5}$	$\frac{4}{7}$ $+\frac{2}{9}$

Problem-Solving Strategy: Solve Multi-Step Problems

Babies gain an average of $2\frac{1}{5}$ pounds each month for the first three months after they are born. Matt weighs $7\frac{1}{2}$ pounds at birth. How much will he probably weigh in 3 months?

Understand the problem.

- **What do you want to know?**
  Matt's weight after 3 months

- **What information is given?**
  He weighs $7\frac{1}{2}$ pounds at birth.
  He gains about $2\frac{1}{5}$ pounds each of the 3 months.

Plan how to solve it.

- **What strategy can you use?**
  You can separate the problem into steps.

Solve it.

- **How can you use this strategy to solve the problem?**
  First find the total weight Matt will gain in the 3 months.
  Then add that total to his birth weight.

Step 1	Step 2
$2\frac{1}{5} \times 3 = \frac{11}{5} \times \frac{3}{1} = \frac{33}{5} = 6\frac{3}{5}$ **Total weight gain $= 6\frac{3}{5}$ pounds**	$\begin{aligned} 7\frac{1}{2} &= 7\frac{5}{10} \\ + 6\frac{3}{5} &= 6\frac{6}{10} \\ \hline &= 13\frac{11}{10} = 14\frac{1}{10} \text{ pounds} \end{aligned}$

- **What is the answer?**
  Matt will probably weigh $14\frac{1}{10}$ pounds in 3 months.

Look back and check your answer.

- **Is your answer reasonable?**
  You can add to check your multiplication.

$$7\frac{1}{2} + 2\frac{1}{5} + 2\frac{1}{5} + 2\frac{1}{5} = 14\frac{1}{10}$$

The answer matches the sum.
The answer is reasonable.

Separate each problem into steps to solve.

1. On average, a baby's head grows $\frac{1}{2}$ inch every month for the first 4 months after birth. Then, from 4 months old to 1 year old, it grows another 2 inches. How many inches does a baby's head grow the first year after it is born? (1 year = 12 months)

Answer _____

2. A recipe for 1 batch of sugar cookies needs $\frac{3}{4}$ tablespoon of vanilla. One batch of lemon cookies needs $\frac{1}{2}$ tablespoon of vanilla. If Ken makes 2 batches of sugar cookies and $\frac{1}{2}$ a batch of lemon cookies, how much vanilla does he need in all?

Answer _____

3. The average person dreams for $\frac{1}{4}$ of the time he or she sleeps. If Anna sleeps for 8 hours, and Brian sleeps for 9 hours, how much longer does Brian dream?

Answer _____

4. Mei earns $8 an hour at the coffee shop. She worked $7\frac{1}{2}$ hours on Saturday and $5\frac{1}{4}$ hours on Sunday. How much money did she earn for the 2 days altogether?

Answer _____

5. United States athletes set the world records for the top three long jumps. The third longest was $29\frac{1}{12}$ feet. The second longest was $\frac{2}{3}$ foot longer than the third. The world's longest jump was $\frac{2}{3}$ foot longer than the second. What was the world record for the longest long jump?

Answer _____

6. Antoine mixed $1\frac{1}{4}$ gallons of blue paint with $\frac{4}{5}$ gallon of yellow paint to make green. Then he mixed $1\frac{3}{4}$ gallons of red paint with $\frac{1}{2}$ gallon of white paint to make pink. Which color did Antoine mix the most of, green or pink?

Answer _____

Problem-Solving Applications

Solve.

1. Kathryn bought $6\frac{1}{2}$ yards of material at $4 per yard. What was the total cost of the material?

   Answer _____

2. An alligator's tail is usually half its total length. If an alligator is $10\frac{1}{4}$ feet long, how long is its tail?

   Answer _____

3. Tim had $2\frac{3}{4}$ feet of wood. He used $\frac{1}{4}$ of the wood to build a frame. How much wood did he use?

   Answer _____

4. Each O in the HOLLYWOOD sign in California is $39\frac{3}{4}$ inches wide. What is the total width of all the O's in the sign?

   Answer _____

5. Kenya put mushrooms on half of her pizza. She ate $\frac{3}{4}$ of the pieces with mushrooms. If the pizza had 8 slices, how many did Kenya eat?

   Answer _____

6. The United States flag has 50 stars. In 1795, the flag had $\frac{3}{10}$ as many stars as today. How many stars were on the 1795 U.S. flag?

   Answer _____

7. In an orchestra, $\frac{2}{3}$ of the musicians play a string instrument. If there are 90 musicians in the orchestra, how many play a string instrument?

   Answer _____

8. Teresa has a 50-acre farm. She plants $\frac{2}{3}$ of her farmland with corn and the rest with tomatoes. How many acres of tomatoes are on Teresa's farm?

   Answer _____

Finding Reciprocals

To divide by a fraction, you need to know how to find reciprocals. **Reciprocals** are numbers whose numerators and denominators have been **inverted,** or switched. The product of two reciprocals is 1.

Write the reciprocals.

$\frac{3}{4}$ reciprocal $= \frac{4}{3}$	$\frac{1}{5}$ reciprocal $= \frac{5}{1} = 5$	$7 = \frac{7}{1}$ reciprocal $= \frac{1}{7}$

PRACTICE

Write the reciprocal.

	a	b	c	d	e
1.	$\frac{2}{3}$ $\frac{3}{2}$	$\frac{1}{6}$	$\frac{7}{8}$	$\frac{5}{9}$	8
2.	$\frac{8}{3}$	12	$\frac{1}{10}$	$\frac{1}{2}$	$\frac{5}{6}$
3.	$\frac{3}{5}$	$\frac{9}{13}$	$\frac{7}{4}$	25	$\frac{1}{4}$

Write as an improper fraction. Then write the reciprocal.

	a	b	c	d
4.	$4\frac{1}{3} =$ $\frac{13}{3}$ $\frac{3}{13}$	$2\frac{4}{5}$	$1\frac{7}{9}$	$5\frac{1}{4}$
5.	$3\frac{2}{3}$	$6\frac{1}{5}$	$10\frac{1}{2}$	$2\frac{7}{9}$
6.	$5\frac{1}{11}$	$1\frac{8}{13}$	$6\frac{1}{8}$	$3\frac{5}{6}$

Write the missing factor.

	a	b	c	d
7.	$\frac{7}{9} \times \frac{9}{7} = 1$	$\frac{1}{5} \times \quad = 1$	$9 \times \quad = 1$	$3\frac{1}{2} \times \quad = 1$

Division of Fractions by Fractions

To divide a fraction by a fraction, multiply by the reciprocal of the second fraction. Simplify the answer if needed. Remember, only the second fraction is inverted.

Find: $\frac{5}{8} \div \frac{3}{4}$

Multiply by the reciprocal of the second fraction.	Cancel.	Multiply the new numerators and denominators.
$\frac{5}{8} \div \frac{3}{4} = \frac{5}{8} \times \frac{4}{3}$	$\frac{5}{\overset{}{\underset{2}{8}}} \times \frac{\overset{1}{4}}{3}$	$\frac{5 \times 1}{2 \times 3} = \frac{5}{6}$

GUIDED PRACTICE

Divide. Simplify.

a

1. $\frac{2}{3} \div \frac{5}{7} = \frac{2}{3} \times \frac{7}{5} = \frac{2 \times 7}{3 \times 5} = \frac{14}{15}$

b

$\frac{3}{8} \div \frac{1}{3} = \frac{3}{8} \times \frac{3}{1} = \frac{3 \times 3}{8 \times 1} =$

2. $\frac{3}{5} \div \frac{2}{3} = \frac{3}{5} \times \frac{3}{2} = \frac{3 \times 3}{5 \times 2} =$

$\frac{8}{9} \div \frac{1}{4} = \frac{8}{9} \times \frac{4}{1} = \frac{8 \times 4}{9 \times 1} =$

3. $\frac{1}{3} \div \frac{1}{8} = \frac{1}{3} \times \frac{8}{1} =$

$\frac{5}{6} \div \frac{4}{5} = \frac{5}{6} \times \frac{5}{4} =$

4. $\frac{3}{8} \div \frac{3}{16} = \frac{3}{8} \times \frac{16}{3} =$

$\frac{7}{10} \div \frac{7}{30} = \frac{7}{10} \times \frac{30}{7} =$

5. $\frac{8}{15} \div \frac{16}{45} = \frac{8}{15} \times \qquad =$

$\frac{9}{16} \div \frac{3}{8} = \frac{9}{16} \times \qquad =$

6. $\frac{5}{12} \div \frac{3}{11} = \frac{5}{12} \times \qquad =$

$\frac{6}{20} \div \frac{4}{15} = \frac{6}{20} \times \qquad =$

Divide. Simplify.

	a	b	c
1.	$\frac{1}{12} \div \frac{1}{4} =$	$\frac{1}{6} \div \frac{1}{6} =$	$\frac{1}{2} \div \frac{3}{8} =$
2.	$\frac{1}{16} \div \frac{1}{12} =$	$\frac{1}{8} \div \frac{1}{16} =$	$\frac{3}{4} \div \frac{5}{8} =$
3.	$\frac{4}{5} \div \frac{1}{10} =$	$\frac{5}{12} \div \frac{3}{4} =$	$\frac{1}{5} \div \frac{1}{20} =$
4.	$\frac{1}{4} \div \frac{4}{9} =$	$\frac{5}{8} \div \frac{5}{8} =$	$\frac{5}{12} \div \frac{3}{2} =$
5.	$\frac{3}{10} \div \frac{1}{10} =$	$\frac{7}{12} \div \frac{3}{8} =$	$\frac{11}{32} \div \frac{5}{16} =$
6.	$\frac{15}{16} \div \frac{3}{5} =$	$\frac{17}{18} \div \frac{2}{3} =$	$\frac{11}{12} \div \frac{1}{6} =$

MIXED PRACTICE

Divide.

	a	b	c	d
1.	$22\overline{)2,0\ 5\ 5}$	$87\overline{)8,9\ 6\ 5}$	$25\overline{)5,7\ 6\ 0}$	$42\overline{)9,1\ 3\ 6}$

Multiply.

	a	b	c	d
2.	$\begin{array}{r} 4\ 1\ 5 \\ \times\ \ \ 2\ 4 \\ \hline \end{array}$	$\begin{array}{r} 3\ 6\ 1 \\ \times\ \ \ 7\ 5 \\ \hline \end{array}$	$\begin{array}{r} 1\ 4\ 9 \\ \times\ \ \ 9\ 4 \\ \hline \end{array}$	$\begin{array}{r} 5\ 3\ 6 \\ \times\ \ \ 2\ 5 \\ \hline \end{array}$

Division of Fractions by Whole Numbers

To divide a fraction by a whole number, multiply by the reciprocal of the whole number. Simplify the quotient. Remember, the reciprocal of a whole number is 1 divided by that number.

Find: $\frac{3}{4} \div 12$

Multiply by the reciprocal of the whole number.	Cancel.	Multiply.
$\frac{3}{4} \times \frac{1}{12}$	$\overset{1}{\cancel{\frac{3}{4}}} \times \frac{1}{\underset{4}{\cancel{12}}}$	$\frac{1 \times 1}{4 \times 4} = \frac{1}{16}$

GUIDED PRACTICE

Divide. Simplify.

a

1. $\frac{5}{8} \div 10 = \overset{1}{\cancel{\frac{5}{8}}} \times \frac{1}{\underset{2}{\cancel{10}}} = \frac{1 \times 1}{8 \times 2} = \frac{1}{16}$

b

$\frac{3}{4} \div 6 = \frac{3}{4} \times \frac{1}{6} =$

2. $\frac{4}{5} \div 20 = \frac{4}{5} \times \frac{1}{20} =$

$\frac{7}{10} \div 14 = \frac{7}{10} \times \frac{1}{14} =$

3. $\frac{7}{8} \div 14 = \frac{7}{8} \times \frac{1}{14} =$

$\frac{9}{20} \div 9 = \frac{9}{20} \times \frac{1}{9} =$

4. $\frac{1}{2} \div 4 = \frac{1}{2} \times \frac{1}{4} =$

$\frac{4}{5} \div 2 = \frac{4}{5} \times \frac{1}{2} =$

5. $\frac{3}{8} \div 6 = \frac{3}{8} \times \frac{1}{6} =$

$\frac{5}{6} \div 4 = \frac{5}{6} \times \frac{1}{4} =$

6. $\frac{3}{4} \div 2 = \frac{3}{4} \times \qquad =$

$\frac{7}{15} \div 7 = \frac{7}{15} \times \qquad =$

7. $\frac{2}{3} \div 8 = \frac{2}{3} \times \qquad =$

$\frac{3}{10} \div 15 = \frac{3}{10} \times \qquad =$

Unit 3 Multiplication and Division of Fractions

PRACTICE

Divide. Simplify.

	a	b	c
1.	$\frac{7}{8} \div 4 =$	$\frac{11}{12} \div 11 =$	$\frac{2}{3} \div 6 =$
2.	$\frac{4}{5} \div 20 =$	$\frac{3}{8} \div 24 =$	$\frac{3}{4} \div 24 =$
3.	$\frac{6}{7} \div 18 =$	$\frac{7}{10} \div 21 =$	$\frac{5}{12} \div 20 =$
4.	$\frac{7}{8} \div 28 =$	$\frac{5}{6} \div 30 =$	$\frac{8}{15} \div 16 =$
5.	$\frac{15}{16} \div 5 =$	$\frac{2}{15} \div 8 =$	$\frac{4}{13} \div 20 =$
6.	$\frac{7}{10} \div 35 =$	$\frac{11}{12} \div 33 =$	$\frac{21}{25} \div 14 =$

MIXED PRACTICE

Find each answer.

	a	b	c	d
1.	$\begin{array}{r} 52,640 \\ +\ \ 8,206 \end{array}$	$\begin{array}{r} 208 \\ \times\ \ \ 45 \end{array}$	$\begin{array}{r} 78,648 \\ -\ \ 1,927 \end{array}$	$\begin{array}{r} 343 \\ \times\ \ 29 \end{array}$
2.	$34\overline{)14,090}$	$17\overline{)4,503}$	$\begin{array}{r} 401,049 \\ -\ \ 23,503 \end{array}$	$\begin{array}{r} 2,307,655 \\ +\ \ 456,923 \end{array}$

Division of Whole Numbers by Fractions

To divide a whole number by a fraction, write the whole number as an improper fraction. Multiply by the reciprocal of the second fraction. Simplify the answer.

Find: $12 \div \frac{3}{4}$

Write the whole number as an improper fraction.	Multiply by the reciprocal of the second fraction.	Cancel.	Multiply and simplify.
$12 \div \frac{3}{4} = \frac{12}{1} \div \frac{3}{4}$	$\frac{12}{1} \times \frac{4}{3}$	$\frac{\overset{4}{\cancel{12}}}{1} \times \frac{4}{\underset{1}{\cancel{3}}}$	$\frac{4 \times 4}{1 \times 1} = \frac{16}{1} = 16$

PRACTICE

Divide. Simplify.

a

1. $10 \div \frac{4}{5} = \frac{10}{1} \div \frac{4}{5} = \frac{\overset{5}{\cancel{10}}}{1} \times \frac{5}{\underset{2}{\cancel{4}}} = \frac{25}{2} = 12\frac{1}{2}$

b

    $5 \div \frac{2}{3} =$

2. $3 \div \frac{3}{4} =$ $3 \div \frac{6}{7} =$

3. $4 \div \frac{2}{7} =$ $6 \div \frac{2}{5} =$

4. $9 \div \frac{3}{4} =$ $9 \div \frac{6}{11} =$

5. $3 \div \frac{15}{16} =$ $27 \div \frac{9}{10} =$

6. $25 \div \frac{4}{5} =$ $15 \div \frac{5}{9} =$

7. $4 \div \frac{1}{2} =$ $2 \div \frac{2}{9} =$

8. $14 \div \frac{3}{7} =$ $8 \div \frac{2}{3} =$

Division of Mixed Numbers by Whole Numbers

To divide a mixed number by a whole number, write the mixed number as an improper fraction. Multiply by the reciprocal of the whole number. Simplify the answer.

Find: $2\frac{1}{3} \div 7$

Write the mixed number as an improper fraction.	Multiply by the reciprocal of the whole number.	Cancel.	Multiply and simplify.
$2\frac{1}{3} \div 7 = \frac{7}{3} \div \frac{7}{1}$	$\frac{7}{3} \times \frac{1}{7}$	$\frac{\overset{1}{\cancel{7}}}{3} \times \frac{1}{\underset{1}{\cancel{7}}}$	$\frac{1 \times 1}{3 \times 1} = \frac{1}{3}$

PRACTICE

Divide. Simplify.

	a	b	c
1.	$3\frac{1}{3} \div 5 =$	$2\frac{1}{2} \div 5 =$	$7\frac{1}{2} \div 3 =$
	$\frac{10}{3} \div \frac{5}{1} = \frac{\overset{2}{\cancel{10}}}{3} \times \frac{1}{\underset{1}{\cancel{5}}} = \frac{2}{3}$		
2.	$6\frac{2}{3} \div 10 =$	$4\frac{1}{5} \div 3 =$	$5\frac{1}{4} \div 7 =$
3.	$6\frac{2}{3} \div 5 =$	$4\frac{1}{6} \div 10 =$	$1\frac{7}{8} \div 5 =$
4.	$4\frac{4}{9} \div 20 =$	$5\frac{5}{9} \div 30 =$	$8\frac{1}{10} \div 9 =$
5.	$7\frac{1}{5} \div 6 =$	$2\frac{1}{12} \div 15 =$	$8\frac{2}{3} \div 39 =$
6.	$3\frac{4}{7} \div 10 =$	$4\frac{1}{8} \div 11 =$	$5\frac{1}{3} \div 24 =$

Division of Mixed Numbers by Fractions

To divide a mixed number by a fraction, write the mixed number as an improper fraction. Multiply by the reciprocal of the second fraction. Simplify the answer.

Find: $1\frac{3}{4} \div \frac{3}{8}$

Write the mixed number as an improper fraction.	Multiply by the reciprocal of the second fraction.	Cancel.	Multiply and simplify.
$1\frac{3}{4} \div \frac{3}{8} = \frac{7}{4} \div \frac{3}{8}$	$\frac{7}{4} \times \frac{8}{3}$	$\frac{7}{\cancel{4}_{1}} \times \frac{\cancel{8}^{2}}{3}$	$\frac{7 \times 2}{1 \times 3} = \frac{14}{3} = 4\frac{2}{3}$

PRACTICE

Divide. Simplify.

a	*b*	*c*
1. $2\frac{1}{3} \div \frac{1}{3} =$	$4\frac{1}{2} \div \frac{1}{2} =$	$3\frac{1}{9} \div \frac{2}{9} =$
$\frac{7}{3} \div \frac{1}{3} = \frac{7}{\cancel{3}_{1}} \times \frac{\cancel{3}^{1}}{1} = \frac{7}{1} = 7$		
2. $6\frac{5}{8} \div \frac{3}{4} =$	$3\frac{5}{8} \div \frac{1}{4} =$	$1\frac{7}{12} \div \frac{5}{6} =$
3. $5\frac{3}{4} \div \frac{1}{8} =$	$10\frac{4}{5} \div \frac{7}{10} =$	$2\frac{3}{8} \div \frac{19}{21} =$
4. $8\frac{3}{4} \div \frac{9}{16} =$	$10\frac{2}{5} \div \frac{2}{3} =$	$2\frac{5}{8} \div \frac{2}{7} =$
5. $3\frac{1}{7} \div \frac{4}{11} =$	$2\frac{3}{10} \div \frac{4}{5} =$	$5\frac{1}{7} \div \frac{5}{14} =$
6. $2\frac{3}{4} \div \frac{8}{9} =$	$4\frac{7}{8} \div \frac{7}{8} =$	$4\frac{3}{5} \div \frac{7}{10} =$

Division of Mixed Numbers by Mixed Numbers

To divide a mixed number by a mixed number, write both mixed numbers as improper fractions. Multiply by the reciprocal of the second fraction. Simplify the answer.

Find: $4\frac{3}{4} \div 1\frac{1}{8}$

Write the mixed numbers as improper fractions.	Multiply by the reciprocal of the second fraction.	Cancel.	Multiply and simplify.
$4\frac{3}{4} \div 1\frac{1}{8} = \frac{19}{4} \div \frac{9}{8}$	$\frac{19}{4} \times \frac{8}{9}$	$\frac{19}{\overset{}{\underset{1}{4}}} \times \frac{\overset{2}{8}}{9}$	$\frac{19 \times 2}{1 \times 9} = \frac{38}{9} = 4\frac{2}{9}$

PRACTICE

Divide. Simplify.

       a   *b*

1. $4\frac{2}{3} \div 3\frac{1}{2} = \frac{14}{3} \div \frac{7}{2} = \frac{14}{3} \times \frac{2}{\underset{1}{7}} = \frac{4}{3} = 1\frac{1}{3}$ $16\frac{2}{3} \div 2\frac{1}{2} =$

2. $6\frac{2}{3} \div 6\frac{1}{4} =$ $6\frac{2}{3} \div 1\frac{1}{4} =$

3. $6\frac{2}{5} \div 5\frac{1}{3} =$ $1\frac{1}{5} \div 2\frac{1}{6} =$

4. $6\frac{2}{3} \div 2\frac{1}{8} =$ $3\frac{1}{10} \div 10\frac{1}{3} =$

5. $2\frac{1}{4} \div 3\frac{3}{8} =$ $2\frac{4}{5} \div 1\frac{2}{5} =$

6. $4\frac{2}{3} \div 5\frac{3}{5} =$ $1\frac{1}{9} \div 2\frac{2}{3} =$

Problem-Solving Strategy: Write a Number Sentence

Some people measure the height of a horse in hands. One inch equals $\frac{1}{4}$ hand. An average Clydesdale horse is 16 hands high. How tall is a Clydesdale in inches?

Understand the problem.

- **What do you want to know?**
  the height of a Clydesdale in inches

- **What information is given?**
  An average Clydesdale horse is 16 hands high.
  1 inch $= \frac{1}{4}$ hand

Plan how to solve it.

- **What strategy can you use?**
  You can write a number sentence to model the problem.

- **How can you use this strategy to solve the problem?**
  You want to know how many groups of $\frac{1}{4}$ hand can be divided into the total 16 hands. Write a division number sentence.

16	$\div$	$\frac{1}{4}$	$=$	_____
↑		↑		↑
total height in hands		number of hands in 1 inch		total height in inches

- **What is the answer?**

  $16 \div \frac{1}{4} = \frac{16}{1} \times \frac{4}{1} = 64$

  An average Clydesdale horse is 64 inches tall.

Look back and check your answer.

- **Is your answer reasonable?**
  You can check division with multiplication.

  64 inches $\times \frac{1}{4} = \frac{64}{1} \times \frac{1}{4} = \frac{64}{4} = 16$ **hands**

  The product matches the dividend.
  The answer is reasonable.

Write a number sentence to solve each problem.

1. Sam had $1\frac{3}{16}$ yards of ribbon. He cut it into pieces $\frac{1}{8}$ of a yard long. How many pieces did he cut?

   Answer _____

2. Fresh apples float because $\frac{1}{4}$ of their weight is air. If a bag of apples weighs $2\frac{1}{2}$ pounds, how many pounds is air?

   Answer _____

3. During its lifetime, one honeybee makes $\frac{1}{12}$ teaspoon of honey. How many honeybees are needed to make $\frac{1}{2}$ teaspoon of honey?

   Answer _____

4. Cheryl has 30 pounds of clay. Each of the refrigerator magnets she is making uses $\frac{3}{4}$ pound of clay. How many magnets can she make?

   Answer _____

5. Yuma, Arizona, and Las Vegas, Nevada, are the two driest cities in the United States. Yuma gets an average of $2\frac{2}{3}$ inches of rain each year. Las Vegas gets about $4\frac{1}{5}$ inches. How many inches does it rain each year in the two cities combined?

   Answer _____

6. The world's tallest dog was a great dane that was $3\frac{5}{11}$ feet tall. The world's smallest dog was a Yorkshire terrier. It was only $\frac{2}{9}$ foot tall. What was the difference between the heights of the two dogs?

   Answer _____

Problem-Solving Applications

Solve.

1. The average giant tortoise walks $\frac{1}{5}$ mile per hour. How many hours will it take a giant tortoise to walk 3 miles?

   Answer _____

2. A recipe for cookies calls for $\frac{3}{4}$ cup of flour. How much flour is needed to make half of the recipe?

   Answer _____

3. The average life span of a grizzly bear is 25 years. A lion usually lives about $\frac{3}{5}$ as long as a grizzly bear. What is the average life span of a lion?

   Answer _____

4. The telephone company evenly placed 6 poles on a $\frac{3}{4}$-mile long street. How far apart were the poles placed?

   Answer _____

5. A peck is $\frac{1}{4}$ of a bushel. If you buy 3 bushels of crabs, how many pecks do you buy?

   Answer _____

6. Most Shetland ponies are 11 hands high. One inch equals $\frac{1}{4}$ hand. How many inches tall are most Shetland ponies?

   Answer _____

7. Rob bought $1\frac{1}{4}$ pounds of ham for $3 per pound. Gina bought $\frac{3}{4}$ pound of turkey for $4 per pound. Who spent more money?

   Answer _____

8. Carrie has 3 United States coins. One of the coins is worth $\frac{1}{20}$ of a dollar. One is worth $\frac{1}{10}$ of a dollar, and the third coin is worth $\frac{1}{100}$ of a dollar. What 3 coins does Carrie have?

   Answer _____

Write each whole number as a fraction.

	a	b	c	d	e	f
1.	$19 =$	$3 =$	$25 =$	$16 =$	$17 =$	$4 =$

Multiply. Use cancellation if possible. Simplify.

	a	b	c
2.	$\frac{2}{5} \times \frac{2}{3} =$	$\frac{2}{3} \times \frac{1}{7} =$	$\frac{1}{2} \times \frac{5}{8} =$
3.	$\frac{1}{2} \times \frac{3}{4} =$	$\frac{5}{6} \times \frac{3}{4} =$	$\frac{2}{8} \times \frac{1}{4} =$
4.	$\frac{15}{16} \times 4 =$	$12 \times \frac{3}{4} =$	$\frac{1}{6} \times 26 =$
5.	$20 \times \frac{2}{5} =$	$24 \times \frac{7}{10} =$	$\frac{2}{3} \times 15 =$
6.	$5\frac{1}{2} \times 3 =$	$3 \times 4\frac{1}{5} =$	$3\frac{1}{4} \times 2 =$
7.	$3\frac{1}{3} \times 4 =$	$9 \times 4\frac{2}{3} =$	$10\frac{1}{5} \times 4 =$
8.	$6\frac{1}{4} \times \frac{3}{5} =$	$\frac{3}{8} \times 4\frac{4}{5} =$	$\frac{1}{6} \times 2\frac{3}{8} =$
9.	$1\frac{3}{7} \times \frac{1}{5} =$	$\frac{5}{9} \times 2\frac{1}{2} =$	$\frac{4}{5} \times 5\frac{1}{4} =$
10.	$5\frac{1}{3} \times 3\frac{3}{8} =$	$4\frac{3}{5} \times 2\frac{3}{7} =$	$1\frac{1}{2} \times 8\frac{3}{4} =$
11.	$1\frac{4}{7} \times 4\frac{1}{2} =$	$3\frac{2}{3} \times 3\frac{1}{5} =$	$4\frac{1}{4} \times 6\frac{2}{3} =$

Write the reciprocal.

	a	b	c	d	e	f

12. $\frac{1}{7}$ _____ $\frac{5}{12}$ _____ $\frac{4}{9}$ _____ $2\frac{3}{7}$ _____ $\frac{2}{15}$ _____ 6 _____

Divide. Use cancellation if possible. Simplify.

	a	b	c

13. $\frac{1}{4} \div \frac{1}{8} =$ $\frac{3}{5} \div \frac{1}{5} =$ $\frac{3}{10} \div \frac{2}{7} =$

14. $\frac{2}{3} \div \frac{3}{7} =$ $\frac{1}{9} \div \frac{4}{5} =$ $\frac{4}{11} \div \frac{1}{8} =$

15. $\frac{13}{24} \div 6 =$ $\frac{5}{9} \div 18 =$ $\frac{6}{15} \div 5 =$

16. $\frac{3}{4} \div 12 =$ $\frac{3}{25} \div 9 =$ $\frac{5}{6} \div 10 =$

17. $15 \div \frac{3}{7} =$ $2 \div \frac{1}{12} =$ $7 \div \frac{4}{11} =$

18. $30 \div \frac{2}{5} =$ $18 \div \frac{3}{4} =$ $100 \div \frac{3}{10} =$

19. $7\frac{1}{5} \div 15 =$ $5\frac{3}{4} \div 12 =$ $2\frac{7}{8} \div 20 =$

20. $3\frac{5}{7} \div \frac{13}{15} =$ $6\frac{2}{3} \div \frac{7}{9} =$ $4\frac{1}{2} \div \frac{3}{12} =$

21. $12\frac{1}{2} \div 2\frac{3}{4} =$ $6\frac{2}{5} \div 5\frac{1}{3} =$ $4\frac{5}{6} \div 3\frac{4}{7} =$

22. $2\frac{1}{9} \div 7\frac{3}{8} =$ $8\frac{1}{3} \div 1\frac{3}{5} =$ $9\frac{4}{6} \div 3\frac{3}{9} =$

Separate each problem into steps to solve.

23. Sara made hot chocolate mix to give to her neighbors. She mixed $4\frac{1}{4}$ cups of sugar with $2\frac{1}{4}$ cups of cocoa. Then she poured $1\frac{1}{2}$ cups of the mix in each jar. How many jars did she fill?

Answer _____

24. The eucalyptus is the world's fastest growing tree. It grows an average of $2\frac{1}{2}$ centimeters every day. If a eucalyptus tree is 50 centimeters tall when it is planted, how tall will it be in 5 days?

Answer _____

Write a number sentence to solve each problem.

25. Maya runs $3\frac{1}{2}$ miles around the track every morning. One lap around the track is $\frac{1}{8}$ mile. How many times does she run around the track every morning?

Answer _____

26. Will completed $\frac{1}{3}$ of his passes during the football season. If he threw 90 passes, how many did he complete?

Answer _____

27. The three-toed sloth is one of the world's slowest animals. It only travels $\frac{1}{20}$ of a mile per hour. How far can a three-toed sloth move in 4 hours?

Answer _____

28. In the frog-jumping contest, the winner jumped $10\frac{4}{5}$ feet. The second-placed frog jumped $9\frac{3}{4}$ feet. What was the difference in the length of their jumps?

Answer _____

Reading and Writing Decimals

To read a **decimal,** read as a whole number.
Then name the place value of the last digit.

Read and write 0.246 as two hundred
forty-six thousandths.

To read a decimal that has a whole number part,
- read the whole number part.
- read the **decimal point** as *and*.
- read the decimal part as a whole
  number then name the place
  value of the last digit.

Read and write 37.05 as thirty-seven and
five hundredths.

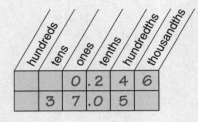

← whole numbers . decimals →

PRACTICE

Write as a decimal.

a   b

1. two tenths _____ *0.2* _____   two hundredths _____

2. two thousandths _____   six and two hundredths _____

3. twenty-one thousandths _____   one and one thousandths _____

Write each decimal in words.

4. 8.07 _____ *eight and seven hundredths* _____

5. 53.009 _____

6. 76.12 _____

Write each money amount with a dollar sign and a decimal point.

a   b   c

7. six dollars _____ *$6.00* _____   sixty cents _____   six cents _____

8. ninety-nine cents _____   twelve cents _____   thirty-one dollars _____

9. four hundred twenty dollars and five cents _____

10. three thousand dollars and ninety-eight cents _____

Comparing and Ordering Decimals

To compare two decimal numbers, begin at the left.
Compare the digits in each place.

The symbol > means **is greater than.** $0.54 > $0.37

The symbol < means **is less than.**   0.829 < 0.84

The symbol = means **is equal to.**   0.23 = 0.230

Compare: 4.1 and 4.3

The ones digits are the same. Compare the tenths.

1 < 3, so 4.1 < 4.3

Compare: $0.52 and $0.09

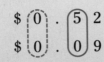

The ones digits are the same. Compare the tenths.

5 > 0, so $0.52 > $0.09

Compare: 7.5 and 7.52

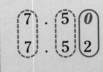

The ones and tenths digits are the same. Write a zero. Compare the hundredths.

0 < 2, so 7.5 < 7.52

PRACTICE

Compare. Write <, >, or =. Write in zeros as needed.

	a	b	c
1.	0.6 __<__ 0.8	0.4 _____ 0.44	0.061 _____ 0.16

```
0 . 6
0 . 8
```

2. $5.25 _____ $5.50 $4.99 _____ $4.98 $0.83 _____ $0.65

```
$5 . 2 5
$5 . 5 0
```

3. 8.9 _____ 8.90   1.36 _____ 1.365   0.921 _____ 0.29

```
8 . 9
8 . 9 0
```

Write in order from least to greatest.

a

4. 0.42   0.4   0.2 __0.2   0.4   0.42__

```
0 . 4 2
0 . 4
0 . 2
```

b

0.31   0.13   0.031 _____

5. 8.1   0.081   0.18 _____   275   2.75   27.5 _____

Fraction and Decimal Equivalents

Sometimes you will need to either change a decimal to a fraction or a fraction to a decimal.

To write a decimal as a fraction, identify the value of the last place in the decimal. Use this place value to write the denominator.

Decimal		Fraction or Mixed Number
0.<u>3</u>	=	$\frac{3}{10}$
0.0<u>5</u>	=	$\frac{5}{100}$
0.03<u>6</u>	=	$\frac{36}{1,000}$
1.9<u>8</u>	=	$\frac{198}{100}$ or $1\frac{98}{100}$

To write a fraction that has a denominator of 10, 100, or 1,000 as a decimal, write the digits from the numerator. Then write the decimal point.

Fraction or Mixed Number		Decimal
$\frac{7}{10}$	=	0.7
$\frac{82}{100}$	=	0.82
$\frac{125}{1,000}$	=	0.125
$\frac{805}{100}$ or $8\frac{05}{100}$	=	8.05

PRACTICE

Write each decimal as a fraction.

	a	b	c	d
1.	0.5 $\frac{5}{10}$	0.4 _____	0.2 _____	0.6 _____
2.	0.05 $\frac{5}{100}$	0.04 _____	0.02 _____	0.06 _____

Write each decimal as a mixed number.

	a	b	c	d
3.	2.1 $2\frac{1}{10}$	45.9 _____	31.6 _____	99.9 _____
4.	3.94 $3\frac{94}{100}$	6.25 _____	12.54 _____	10.01 _____

Write each fraction as a decimal.

	a	b	c	d
5.	$\frac{9}{10}$ 0.9	$\frac{3}{10}$ _____	$\frac{1}{10}$ _____	$\frac{8}{10}$ _____
6.	$\frac{7}{100}$ .07	$\frac{91}{100}$ _____	$\frac{63}{1,000}$ _____	$\frac{527}{1,000}$ _____
7.	$\frac{67}{10}$ $6\frac{7}{10} = 6.7$	$\frac{42}{10}$ _____	$\frac{87}{10}$ _____	$\frac{76}{10}$ _____
8.	$\frac{204}{100}$ $2\frac{04}{100} = 2.04$	$\frac{610}{100}$ _____	$\frac{1,754}{1,000}$ _____	$\frac{3,062}{1,000}$ _____

Fraction and Decimal Equivalents

Not all fractions can be changed to **decimal form** easily.
To write fractions that have denominators other than 10, 100, or 1,000 as decimals, first write an equivalent fraction that has a denominator of 10, 100, or 1,000. Then write the equivalent fraction as a decimal.

Remember, not all fractions have simple decimal equivalents.

Examples: $\frac{2}{11} = 0.1818\ldots$ and $\frac{2}{3} = 0.666\ldots$

Write $\frac{3}{4}$ as a decimal.

Write $\frac{3}{4}$ with 100 as the denominator.	Write the fraction as a decimal.
$\frac{3}{4} = \frac{3 \times 25}{4 \times 25} = \frac{75}{100}$	$= 0.75$

Write $2\frac{1}{2}$ as a decimal.

Write $2\frac{1}{2}$ as an improper fraction.	Write the new fraction with 10 as the denominator.	Write the fraction as a decimal.
$2\frac{1}{2} = \frac{5}{2}$	$\frac{5}{2} = \frac{5 \times 5}{2 \times 5} = \frac{25}{10}$	$= 2.5$

PRACTICE

Write each fraction as a decimal.

	a	b	c
1.	$\frac{2}{5} = \dfrac{2 \times 2}{5 \times 2} = \frac{4}{10} = 0.4$	$\frac{1}{4} = $ _____	$\frac{1}{2} = $ _____
2.	$\frac{5}{20} = $ _____	$\frac{5}{25} = $ _____	$\frac{7}{20} = $ _____
3.	$\frac{13}{20} = $ _____	$\frac{17}{25} = $ _____	$\frac{3}{5} = $ _____
4.	$\frac{17}{4} = \dfrac{17 \times 25}{4 \times 25} = \frac{425}{100} = 4.25$	$\frac{7}{2} = $ _____	$\frac{13}{5} = $ _____
5.	$\frac{37}{25} = $ _____	$\frac{43}{20} = $ _____	$\frac{79}{25} = $ _____

Write each mixed number as a decimal.

	a	b
6.	$6\frac{1}{5} = \dfrac{31}{5} = \dfrac{31 \times 2}{5 \times 2} = \frac{62}{10} = 6.2$	$10\frac{3}{4} = $ _____
7.	$3\frac{5}{25} = $ _____	$4\frac{7}{25} = $ _____
8.	$13\frac{1}{2} = $ _____	$7\frac{2}{5} = $ _____

Problem-Solving Strategy: Use Logic

Christine Arron, Florence Griffith-Joyner, and Marion Jones have been considered the fastest-running women on Earth. Their times for the 100-meter dash were 10.73 seconds, $10\frac{13}{20}$ seconds, and 10.49 seconds. Jones's time has a 6 in the tenths place. Griffith-Joyner was faster than Arron. Using this information, determine the fastest runner.

Understand the problem.

- **What do you want to know?**
  the fastest-running woman

- **What information do you know?**
  Their times were 10.73 seconds, $10\frac{13}{20}$ seconds, and 10.49 seconds. The fastest time is the smallest number.
  Clue 1: Jones's time has a 6 in the tenths place.
  Clue 2: Griffith-Joyner was faster than Arron.

Plan how to solve it.

- **What strategy can you use?**
  You can organize all the possibilities in a table.
  Then you can use logic to match the clues to the possibilities.

Solve it.

- **How can you use this strategy to solve the problem?**
  First, change all the times to decimals so they can be compared. Since each of the runners has one time, there can only be one **YES** in each row and column.

	10.73	$10\frac{13}{20} = 10.65$	10.49
Arron	**YES**	no	no
Griffith-Joyner	no	no	**YES**
Jones	no	**YES**	no

- **What is the answer?**
  Florence Griffith-Joyner

Look back and check your answer.

- **Is your answer reasonable?**
  Clue 1: Jones's time has a 6 in the tenths place.
  Clue 2: Griffith-Joyner was faster than Arron.

  The answer matches the clues.
  The answer is reasonable.

  Check:
  10.**6**5
  $10.49 < 10.73$

Use logic to solve each problem.

1. The three largest earthquakes ever recorded took place in Chile, Russia, and Alaska. They measured $9\frac{1}{10}$, 9.5, and $9\frac{1}{5}$ on the Richter scale. The largest earthquake was in Chile. The earthquake in Russia was smaller than the one in Alaska. What did the three earthquakes measure on the Richter scale?

Chile _____

Russia _____

Alaska _____

2. The National Park Service has measured the Statue of Liberty's hand, face, and the tablet she holds. Their lengths are 16.42 feet, $17\frac{1}{4}$ feet, and 25.58 feet. Her hand is the shortest of the three. The length of her face has a 5 in the hundredths place. What are the lengths of the Statue of Liberty's hand, face, and tablet?

hand _____

face _____

tablet _____

3. Jamaal weighs a penny, nickel, and dime on a metric scale. One coin is five and fourteen hundredths grams. The weights of the other two coins are 2.26 grams and $2\frac{3}{5}$ grams. The nickel weighs the most. The weight of the dime has a 6 in the hundredths place. Which coin weighs the least?

Answer_____

4. Alpha Centauri, Barnard's Star, and Proxima Centauri are the three closest stars to Earth. Their distances from Earth are 5.98 light years, $4\frac{7}{20}$ light years, and $4\frac{11}{50}$ light years. Barnard's Star is farthest from Earth. Alpha Centauri's distance from Earth has a 3 in the tenths place. What is the closest star to Earth?

Answer_____

Unit 4 Decimals

Problem-Solving Applications

Solve.

1. The odometer reading on Jennifer's new car was thirty-six and five tenths miles. Write this number using digits.

Answer _____

2. In the 50-meter backstroke race, Bill's time was 30.23 seconds. Sam finished in 30.32 seconds. Who won the race?

Answer _____

3. Kyle picked $2\frac{4}{5}$ pounds of berries. Ali picked 2.75 pounds of berries. Who picked the most berries?

Answer _____

4. The average person in the United States drinks $54\frac{17}{25}$ gallons of soda every year. Write this amount as a decimal.

Answer _____

5. One summer, Ryan earned $126.75. Write this amount using words.

Answer _____

6. Earl's cat weighs 2.75 kilograms. Write this number as a fraction. Simplify.

Answer _____

7. It took a computer forty-six thousandths of a second to print a short message. Write this time using digits.

Answer _____

8. The femur, or thighbone, is the longest human bone. Its average length is $19\frac{22}{25}$ inches. Write its length as a decimal.

Answer _____

Unit 4 Decimals

Rounding Decimals

Round decimals to estimate how many. You can use a number line to round decimals.

Remember, when a number is halfway, always round up.

Round 31.2 to the nearest one.

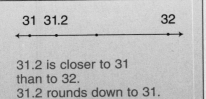

31.2 is closer to 31 than to 32.
31.2 rounds down to 31.

Round $4.67 to the nearest dollar.

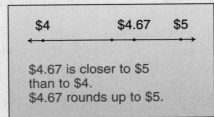

$4.67 is closer to $5 than to $4.
$4.67 rounds up to $5.

Round 6.15 to the nearest tenth.

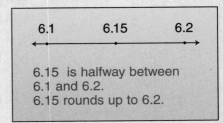

6.15 is halfway between 6.1 and 6.2.
6.15 rounds up to 6.2.

PRACTICE

Round to the nearest one.

	a	b	c	d
1.	4.4 ___4___	3.6 _____	2.5 _____	8.4 _____
2.	43.7 _____	51.5 _____	44.6 _____	73.1 _____
3.	59.5 ___60___	93.4 _____	67.3 _____	40.7 _____
4.	6.39 _____	8.76 _____	5.02 _____	9.93 _____

Round each amount to the nearest dollar.

	a	b	c	d
5.	$3.92 ___$4___	$25.47 _____	$7.92 _____	$6.35 _____
6.	$8.04 _____	$2.56 _____	$9.53 _____	$62.06 _____
7.	$201.63 _____	$0.58 _____	$20.30 _____	$9.99 _____
8.	$1.21 _____	$6.49 _____	$2.95 _____	$8.50 _____

Round to the nearest tenth.

	a	b	c	d
9.	0.58 ___0.6___	0.91 _____	0.64 _____	0.79 _____
10.	4.08 _____	8.67 _____	2.34 _____	9.33 _____
11.	61.97 _____	47.82 _____	99.99 _____	50.95 _____
12.	39.96 ___40___	25.81 _____	72.02 _____	21.63 _____

Addition and Subtraction of Decimals

To add or subtract decimals, line up the decimal points.
Write zeros as needed. Then add or subtract the same way
as whole numbers.

Find: 8.3 + 5.96

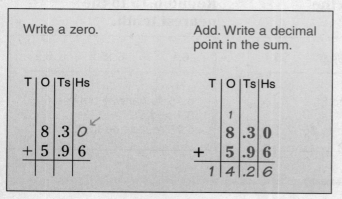

Write a zero.	Add. Write a decimal point in the sum.

T	O	Ts	Hs
	8	.3	0
+ 5	.9	6	

T	O	Ts	Hs
	1		
	8	.3	0
+	5	.9	6
1	4	.2	6

Find: 39.2 − 26.71

Write a zero.	Regroup. Subtract. Write a decimal point in the difference.

T	O	Ts	Hs
3	9	.2	0
− 2	6	.7	1

T	O	Ts	Hs
	8	11	10
3	9	.2	0
− 2	6	.7	1
1	2	.4	9

GUIDED PRACTICE

Add or subtract. Write zeros as needed.

	a	b	c	d

1.

a.
T	O	Ts
1	1	
1	6	.2
+2	4	.9
4	1	.1

b.
T	O	Ts
5	0	.6
+3	8	.4

c.
T	O	Ts
	12	
6	2	11
7	3	.1
−2	5	.3
4	7	.8

d.
T	O	Ts	Hs
$4	8	.5	0
− 3	0	.6	3

2.

a. 2.3 5 6 + 8.6 7 9

b. 4.6 2 9 + 3.4 7 5

c. 2 4.6 1 − 2.8

d. 8 7.5 9 − 4 9

3.

a. $ 4 5.8 5 + 3 2.1 4

b. $ 2 6.1 8 + 1 3.7 5

c. 3.7 5 7 − 0.5 0 9

d. 6 1.0 0 5 − 5 7.3 7 6

4.

a. 1 2 5.8 + 1 7.4 5

b. 2 3 4.6 + 1 9.5 2

c. 3 5.0 8 − 2 4.1 2 6

d. 8 4.7 − 1 7.3 6

5.

a. 2 8.2 4
1 6.4 5
+1 4.2 3

b. 7 8.0 9
2 5.1 0
+2 1 8.4 5

c. 8 − 0.5 2 9

d. 9 6 − 4.0 0 1

PRACTICE

Add or subtract. Write zeros as needed.

	a	*b*	*c*	*d*
1.	5. 4 7 +6. 8 9	7. 5 6 9 +2. 0 8	1 7. 5 3 − 9. 4	2 6. 3 3 −1 5. 8
2.	1 3. 6 − 8. 5 4	6 0. 3 8 +4 2. 9	$ 1. 5 6 − 0. 9 9	$ 2 5. 7 5 + 1 6. 5 9
3.	6 3 1. 2 5 + 9. 7 1	1 8 5. 2 2 − 4 7. 3	6 9. 2 − 5. 1 7	9 8. 6 +3 3. 5
4.	1. 8 +0. 7 5 3	2 6. 1 5 +1 0 0. 8	$ 2 0 − 5. 9 9	$ 8. 6 3 + 1 9. 7 5
5.	3. 8 6. 5 4 +2 1. 8 7	6 1 4. 5 +2 7. 9	1 0 − 1. 5 4	6 −0. 2 9 3

Line up the digits. Then find the sums or differences.

        a   *b*

6. $6.54 + 12.9 =$ _____ $28.3 - 14.65 =$ _____

7. $35 - 4.98 =$ _____ $\$8.99 + \$24.50 =$ _____

Find each answer.

	a	*b*	*c*	*d*
1.	$\frac{3}{4} + \frac{2}{5} =$	$\frac{7}{9} - \frac{1}{3} =$	$\frac{4}{5} \times \frac{1}{6} =$	$\frac{9}{10} \div \frac{1}{2} =$

Estimation of Decimal Sums and Differences

To estimate a decimal sum or difference, first round the decimals to the same place. Then add or subtract the rounded numbers.

Estimate: 7.13 + 2.89

Round each decimal to the nearest one.
Add.

$$
\begin{array}{r}
7.13 \rightarrow 7 \\
+2.89 \rightarrow +\ 3 \\
\hline
10
\end{array}
$$

Estimate: 9.26 − 3.42

Round each decimal to the nearest tenth.
Subtract.

$$
\begin{array}{r}
9.76 \rightarrow 9.8 \\
-3.42 \rightarrow -3.4 \\
\hline
6.4
\end{array}
$$

GUIDED PRACTICE

Estimate each sum or difference by rounding to the nearest one.

	a	b	c	d
1.	$\begin{array}{r} 7.3 \rightarrow 7 \\ +0.6 \rightarrow +\ 1 \\ \hline 8 \end{array}$	$\begin{array}{r} \$\ 2.5\ 6 \rightarrow \\ +\ \ 3.8\ 9 \rightarrow \\ \hline \end{array}$	$\begin{array}{r} \$\ 1\ 3.8\ 4 \rightarrow \\ +\ \ \ \ \ 7.6\ 3 \rightarrow \\ \hline \end{array}$	$\begin{array}{r} 5\ 4.2\ 5 \rightarrow \\ +6\ 2.5\ 1 \rightarrow \\ \hline \end{array}$
2.	$\begin{array}{r} 5.4 \rightarrow 5 \\ -4.6 \rightarrow -\ 5 \\ \hline 0 \end{array}$	$\begin{array}{r} \$\ 6.1\ 8 \rightarrow \\ -\ \ 2.5\ 9 \rightarrow \\ \hline \end{array}$	$\begin{array}{r} \$\ 8\ 2.6\ 4 \rightarrow \\ -\ \ \ 3\ 3.2\ 1 \rightarrow \\ \hline \end{array}$	$\begin{array}{r} 2\ 7.4\ 9 \rightarrow \\ -1\ 9.6\ 0 \rightarrow \\ \hline \end{array}$
3.	$\begin{array}{r} 2.9\ 4 \rightarrow \\ +3.8\ \ \ \rightarrow \\ \hline \end{array}$	$\begin{array}{r} 7.6\ \ \ \rightarrow \\ +5.2\ 7 \rightarrow \\ \hline \end{array}$	$\begin{array}{r} 5\ 3.8\ 7 \rightarrow \\ +1\ 2.9\ \ \ \rightarrow \\ \hline \end{array}$	$\begin{array}{r} 9.2\ \ \ \rightarrow \\ -0.8\ 5 \rightarrow \\ \hline \end{array}$

Estimate each sum or difference by rounding to the nearest tenth.

	a	b	c	d
4.	$\begin{array}{r} 3.6\ 4 \rightarrow 3.6 \\ +2.7\ 8 \rightarrow +2.8 \\ \hline 6.4 \end{array}$	$\begin{array}{r} 5.4\ 5 \rightarrow \\ +1.7\ 4 \rightarrow \\ \hline \end{array}$	$\begin{array}{r} 2\ 7.2\ 6 \rightarrow \\ +1\ 4.3\ 5 \rightarrow \\ \hline \end{array}$	$\begin{array}{r} 3\ 5.6\ 4 \rightarrow \\ +1\ 7.2\ 6 \rightarrow \\ \hline \end{array}$
5.	$\begin{array}{r} 6.9\ 8 \rightarrow 7.0 \\ -1.3\ 7 \rightarrow -\ 1.4 \\ \hline 5.6 \end{array}$	$\begin{array}{r} 4.5\ 6 \rightarrow \\ -2.3\ 1 \rightarrow \\ \hline \end{array}$	$\begin{array}{r} 5\ 8.7\ 3 \rightarrow \\ -2\ 2.4\ 5 \rightarrow \\ \hline \end{array}$	$\begin{array}{r} 6\ 8.7\ 0 \rightarrow \\ -1\ 6.6\ 3 \rightarrow \\ \hline \end{array}$
6.	$\begin{array}{r} 5\ 3.8\ 7 \rightarrow \\ +6\ 2.6\ \ \ \rightarrow \\ \hline \end{array}$	$\begin{array}{r} 4\ 8.6\ \ \ \rightarrow \\ -1\ 2.2\ 3 \rightarrow \\ \hline \end{array}$	$\begin{array}{r} 2.6\ \ \ \rightarrow \\ -0.5\ 9\ 4 \rightarrow \\ \hline \end{array}$	$\begin{array}{r} 7.3\ 6 \rightarrow \\ -0.2\ 4 \rightarrow \\ \hline \end{array}$

PRACTICE

Estimate each sum or difference by rounding to the nearest one.

	a	b	c	d
1.	$4.7 \rightarrow$ $+0.9 \rightarrow$	$1\ 2.3 \rightarrow$ $+\ \ 3.6 \rightarrow$	$2\ 5.1 \rightarrow$ $+1\ 4.5 \rightarrow$	$7\ 4.5 \rightarrow$ $+\ \ 0.9 \rightarrow$
2.	$6.8\ 2 \rightarrow$ $-3.4\ 4 \rightarrow$	$1\ 1.7\ 1 \rightarrow$ $-\ \ 4.8\ 3 \rightarrow$	$8\ 0.9\ 5 \rightarrow$ $-1\ 6.4\ 2 \rightarrow$	$3\ 6.5\ 7 \rightarrow$ $-2\ 0.7\ 9 \rightarrow$
3.	$\$\ 5.6\ 8 \rightarrow$ $+\ \ 0.7\ 5 \rightarrow$	$\$\ 3\ 5.9\ 9 \rightarrow$ $+\ \ 1\ 7.2\ 5 \rightarrow$	$\$\ 9.2\ 4 \rightarrow$ $-\ \ 7.5\ 8 \rightarrow$	$\$\ 8\ 0.6\ 5 \rightarrow$ $-\ \ \ \ 6.9\ 9 \rightarrow$

Estimate each sum or difference by rounding to the nearest tenth.

	a	b	c	d
4.	$6.8\ 4 \rightarrow$ $+1.3\ 7 \rightarrow$	$4.9\ 5 \rightarrow$ $+3.1\ 4 \rightarrow$	$6\ 9.5\ 9 \rightarrow$ $+3\ 1.9\ 6 \rightarrow$	$3\ 7.6\ 1 \rightarrow$ $+\ \ 9.6\ 1 \rightarrow$
5.	$6.5\ 7 \rightarrow$ $-4.4\ 9 \rightarrow$	$8.7\ 8 \rightarrow$ $-2.6\ 5 \rightarrow$	$1\ 7.5\ 2 \rightarrow$ $-\ \ 6.4\ 9 \rightarrow$	$8\ 5.3\ 9 \rightarrow$ $-\ \ 9.1\ 2 \rightarrow$
6.	$\$\ 8.0\ 6 \rightarrow$ $+\ \ 1.3\ 4 \rightarrow$	$\$\ 6\ 4.8\ 5 \rightarrow$ $+\ \ 2\ 9.5\ 6 \rightarrow$	$\$\ 8.7\ 5 \rightarrow$ $-\ \ 3.0\ 7 \rightarrow$	$\$\ 6\ 9.4\ 1 \rightarrow$ $-\ \ 1\ 9.2\ 4 \rightarrow$

MIXED PRACTICE

Find each answer.

	a	b	c	d
1.	$4,9\ 0\ 5$ $-2,6\ 5\ 8$	$2\ 5,1\ 8\ 7$ $+\ \ 9,3\ 4\ 7$	$1\ 7\ 5$ $\times 2\ 6\ 3$	$5\overline{)4,8\ 4\ 5}$

Problem-Solving Strategy: Work Backwards

Jerome has $646.15 in his bank account. During the last two weeks, he withdrew $115.28, deposited $83.30, and withdrew $62.97. How much did Jerome have in his account two weeks ago?

Understand the problem.

- **What do you want to know?**
  How much money was in Jerome's account two weeks ago?

- **What information is given?**
  There is $646.15 in the account now.
  He withdrew $115.28, deposited $83.30, and withdrew $62.97.

Plan how to solve it.

- **What strategy can you use?**
  You can work backwards. Work from the money in the account now to find the money in the account two weeks ago.

Solve it.

- **How can you use this strategy to solve the problem?**
  Addition and subtraction are opposite operations. So, add the amounts withdrawn and subtract the amount deposited.

$$
\begin{array}{rl}
\$646.15 & \leftarrow \text{amount in bank now} \\
+\ 115.28 & \leftarrow \text{amount withdrawn} \\
\hline
\$761.43 & \\
-\ \ \ 83.30 & \leftarrow \text{amount deposited} \\
\hline
\$678.13 & \\
+\ \ \ 62.97 & \leftarrow \text{amount withdrawn} \\
\hline
\$741.10 &
\end{array}
$$

- **What is the answer?**
  Two weeks ago, Jerome had $741.10 in his account.

Look back and check your answer.

- **Is your answer reasonable?**
  You can check by working forwards from the amount of money in the account two weeks ago.

$$
\begin{array}{r}
\$741.10 \\
-\ 115.28 \\
\hline
\$625.82 \\
+\ \ \ 83.30 \\
\hline
\$709.12 \\
-\ \ \ 62.97 \\
\hline
\$646.15
\end{array}
$$

The amount in his account and the answer match.
The answer is reasonable.

Work backwards to solve each problem.

1. Anne has $85.97 left over from her paycheck. She spent $117.43 for insurance and $49.05 for her phone bill. Then she spent $37.28 for groceries. How much was Anne's paycheck?

Answer_____

2. Julio spent $46.00 for a radio. Then he paid $14.00 each for 3 shirts. He had $18.00 left over. How much money did Julio take shopping?

Answer_____

3. Half of the students in Linda's class are girls. Half of the girls have blue eyes. Seven girls have blue eyes. How many students are in Linda's class?

Answer_____

4. Sue is guessing her grandfather's age. He tells her that when you divide his age by 3 and then subtract 7, the result is 13. How old is Sue's grandfather?

Answer_____

5. The park cleanup started at 9:00 A.M. By noon, there were three times more people than had started. At 12:30, another 12 people arrived. Now there are 42 people in all. How many people started at 9:00 A.M.?

Answer_____

6. Gabrielle used 18.5 centimeters of wire to make a bracelet. Then she made 2 earrings using 4.75 centimeters of wire for each one. She had 26.38 centimeters of wire left over. How much wire did Gabrielle start with?

Answer_____

Problem-Solving Applications

Solve.

1. The diameter of an average human hair is 0.078 millimeters. Round this measure to the nearest hundredth of a millimeter.

   Answer _____

2. One centimeter is equal to 0.3937 inches. Round this value to the nearest tenth of an inch.

   Answer _____

3. The Golden Gate Bridge is 2,789.4 meters long. The Mackinac Bridge is 2,255.92 meters long. Which bridge is longer? How much longer?

   Answer _____

4. Three hamsters weighing 2.67 ounces, 2.417 ounces, and 2.59 ounces are in the same cage. What is their combined weight?

   Answer _____

5. Mobile, Alabama, gets about 63.96 inches of rain each year. Astoria, Oregon, gets about 66.4 inches. How much rain do the two cities get each year in all?

   Answer _____

6. The average barn spider is 1.49 inches long. The average garden spider is 0.95 inches long. What is the difference in the lengths of the two spiders?

   Answer _____

7. Lita bought a vase for $7.59 and six roses for $12.35. To the nearest whole dollar, how much did Lita spend?

   Answer _____

8. A day on Jupiter is 9.925 hours. A day on Saturn is 10.673 hours. To the nearest hundredth of an hour, what is the difference in the lengths of their days?

   Answer _____

Write as a decimal.

a   *b*

1. sixty-seven thousandths _____   seventy-six hundredths _____

Write each decimal in words.

2. 42.615 _____

3. 0.078 _____

Write each money amount with a dollar sign and a decimal point.

4. sixty-eight dollars and twenty-seven cents _____

5. four hundred five dollars and three cents _____

Compare. Write <, >, or =. Write in zeros as needed.

           a   *b*   *c*

6. 0.52 _____ 0.25   0.213 _____ 0.123   1.806 _____ 1.860

Write in order from least to greatest.

           a   *b*

7. 0.5   0.052   0.25 _____   0.19   0.91   0.019 _____

Write each decimal as a fraction.

           a   *b*   *c*   *d*

8. 0.3 _____   0.25 _____   0.07 _____   0.8 _____

Write each decimal as a mixed number.

           a   *b*   *c*   *d*

9. 1.75 _____   5.2 _____   24.06 _____   16.75 _____

Write each fraction as a decimal.

           a   *b*   *c*   *d*

10. $\frac{108}{100}$ _____ $\frac{7}{10}$ _____ $\frac{3}{5}$ _____ $\frac{11}{25}$ _____

Write each mixed number as a decimal.

           a   *b*   *c*   *d*

11. $2\frac{7}{10}$ _____ $5\frac{3}{5}$ _____ $10\frac{1}{4}$ _____ $8\frac{3}{4}$ _____

Round to the nearest one.

a	b	c	d
12. 7.6 _____	2.2 _____	3.8 _____	0.5 _____

Round each amount to the nearest dollar.

a	b	c	d
13. $7.95 _____	$4.27 _____	$9.03 _____	$15.49 _____

Round to the nearest tenth.

a	b	c	d
14. 0.38 _____	0.19 _____	5.12 _____	72.09 _____

Add or subtract. Write zeros as needed.

a   b   c   d

15.
$$\begin{array}{r} 4\,2.7 \\ +6\,8.9 \\ \hline \end{array} \qquad \begin{array}{r} 3.0\,0\,1 \\ +0.9\,5\,7 \\ \hline \end{array} \qquad \begin{array}{r} \$\,2\,9.9\,5 \\ +\ \ 5\,6.4\,9 \\ \hline \end{array} \qquad \begin{array}{r} 6\,8.5 \\ +\ \ 0.8\,1\,4 \\ \hline \end{array}$$

16.
$$\begin{array}{r} 2.0\,2 \\ -1.9\,9 \\ \hline \end{array} \qquad \begin{array}{r} 7 \\ -4.5\,8 \\ \hline \end{array} \qquad \begin{array}{r} \$\,1\,1\,2.2\,5 \\ -\ \ \ \ 3\,6.4\,9 \\ \hline \end{array} \qquad \begin{array}{r} 8.0\,1 \\ -0.5\,8 \\ \hline \end{array}$$

17.
$$\begin{array}{r} \$\,1\,6.1\,5 \\ 3\,9.0\,6 \\ +\ \ 3\,4.7\,9 \\ \hline \end{array} \qquad \begin{array}{r} 1 \\ -0.8\,1 \\ \hline \end{array} \qquad \begin{array}{r} 4\,0 \\ -\ \ 0.3\,6\,1 \\ \hline \end{array} \qquad \begin{array}{r} 1\,1\,3.5 \\ 3\,6.9 \\ +2\,0\,7.4\,6 \\ \hline \end{array}$$

Estimate each sum or difference by rounding to the nearest one.

a   b   c   d

18.
$$\begin{array}{r} 4.1 \rightarrow \\ +9.8 \rightarrow \\ \hline \end{array} \qquad \begin{array}{r} 6.5 \rightarrow \\ +3.7 \rightarrow \\ \hline \end{array} \qquad \begin{array}{r} 9\,4.7 \rightarrow \\ -1\,6.4 \rightarrow \\ \hline \end{array} \qquad \begin{array}{r} 1\,1.3\,2 \rightarrow \\ -\ \ 8.2\ \ \rightarrow \\ \hline \end{array}$$

Estimate each sum or difference by rounding to the nearest tenth.

a   b   c   d

19.
$$\begin{array}{r} 1.3\,6 \rightarrow \\ +8.2\,5 \rightarrow \\ \hline \end{array} \qquad \begin{array}{r} 5.6\,4 \rightarrow \\ +7.0\,2 \rightarrow \\ \hline \end{array} \qquad \begin{array}{r} 6.7\,9 \rightarrow \\ -4.1\,4 \rightarrow \\ \hline \end{array} \qquad \begin{array}{r} 2\,5.6\,8 \rightarrow \\ -1\,2.4\,9 \rightarrow \\ \hline \end{array}$$

Use logic to solve each problem.

20. The three fastest times ever recorded for the 100-meter dash were set by Tim Montgomery, Maurice Greene, and Donovan Bailey. Their times for the 100-meter dash are 9.78 seconds, $9\frac{21}{25}$ seconds, and 9.79 seconds. Bailey's time has a 4 in the hundredths place. Montgomery is faster than Greene. Who recorded the world record in the 100-meter dash?

Answer _____

21. The three tallest trees in the United States measure 100.3 meters, 95.4 meters, and $83\frac{22}{25}$ meters. One of the trees is a Douglas fir. The other two trees are a redwood and a giant sequoia. The sequoia has a 4 in the tenths place. The redwood is not the tallest. What are the heights of the three trees?

Douglas fir _____

Redwood _____

Giant sequoia _____

Work backwards to solve each problem.

22. Celia's model train set now has 68.3 feet of tracks. After she bought it, she added 24.65 feet of tracks. But it was too long for the room. She then took off 9.7 feet. How many feet of tracks came with Celia's train set when she bought it?

Answer _____

23. Sean spent a total of $106.43 for the team party. He paid $6.98 for invitations and $74.25 for food and drinks. He spent the rest of the money on decorations. How much did Sean pay for the decorations?

Answer _____

Multiplying by Powers of Ten

To multiply decimals by **powers of ten,** move the decimal point in the product to the right as many places as there are zeros in the multiplier.

Remember, sometimes you might need to write zeros in the product in order to move the decimal point the correct number of places.

Study these examples.

$10 \times 0.24 = 2.4$ $100 \times 0.54 = 54$ $1,000 \times 0.36 = 360$

$10 \times 0.245 = 2.45$ $100 \times 0.545 = 54.5$ $1,000 \times 0.367 = 367$

$10 \times 2.4 = 24$ $100 \times 5.4 = 540$ $1,000 \times 3.670 = 3,670$

$10 \times 2.04 = 20.4$ $100 \times 5.04 = 504$ $1,000 \times 3.067 = 3,067$

PRACTICE

Multiply. Write zeros as needed.

	a	b	c
1.	$0.58 \times 10 =$ ___5.8___	$5.8 \times 10 =$ _____	$0.058 \times 10 =$ _____
2.	$7.5 \times 10 =$ _____	$0.83 \times 10 =$ _____	$4.6 \times 10 =$ _____
3.	$2.8 \times 100 =$ _____	$0.7 \times 100 =$ _____	$0.07 \times 100 =$ _____
4.	$4.6 \times 1,000 =$ _____	$6.2 \times 1,000 =$ _____	$0.075 \times 1,000 =$ _____
5.	$3.1 \times 10 =$ _____	$3.1 \times 100 =$ _____	$3.15 \times 1,000 =$ _____

Multiplying Decimals by Whole Numbers

To multiply decimals by whole numbers, multiply the same way as whole numbers. Place the decimal point in the product by counting the numbers of decimal places in each factor. The product will have the same number of decimal places.

Find: 18 × 2.3

Multiply. Write the decimal point in the product.

```
    2.3        1 decimal place
  × 18        +0 decimal places
  ────
  184
   23
  ────
  41.4        1 decimal place
```

Find: 63 × 0.128

Multiply. Write the decimal point in the product.

```
   0.128       3 decimal places
 ×    63      +0 decimal places
 ─────
   384
   768
 ─────
 8.064         3 decimal places
```

PRACTICE

Multiply. Write zeros as needed.

	a	b	c	d
1.	$\begin{array}{r} 0.2 \\ \times\ 8 \\ \hline 1.6 \end{array}$	$\begin{array}{r} 0.2\,4 \\ \times\quad 4 \\ \hline \end{array}$	$\begin{array}{r} 4.7 \\ \times\ 5 \\ \hline \end{array}$	$\begin{array}{r} 3.0\,9\,2 \\ \times\qquad 6 \\ \hline \end{array}$
2.	$\begin{array}{r} 3\,2 \\ \times 0.0\,4 \\ \hline \end{array}$	$\begin{array}{r} 4\,0\,7 \\ \times\ 2.8 \\ \hline \end{array}$	$\begin{array}{r} 0.2\,3\,1 \\ \times\qquad 4\,7 \\ \hline \end{array}$	$\begin{array}{r} 4\,3\,7 \\ \times 0.0\,0\,2 \\ \hline \end{array}$
3.	$\begin{array}{r} 3.0\,0\,2 \\ \times\qquad 2\,6 \\ \hline \end{array}$	$\begin{array}{r} 0.2\,0\,5 \\ \times\qquad 3\,5 \\ \hline \end{array}$	$\begin{array}{r} 3\,6\,8 \\ \times 0.0\,3\,2 \\ \hline \end{array}$	$\begin{array}{r} 1.1\,0\,1 \\ \times\qquad 8\,0\,9 \\ \hline \end{array}$

Line up the digits. Then find the products. Write zeros as needed.

	a	b	c
4.	$41 \times 15.4 =$ _____	$16 \times 4.3 =$ _____	$112 \times 448.5 =$ _____

$\begin{array}{r} 1\,5.4 \\ \times\quad 4\,1 \\ \hline \end{array}$

Multiplying Decimals by Decimals

To multiply decimals by decimals, multiply the same way as whole numbers. Place the decimal point in the product by counting the number of decimal places in each factor. The product will have the same number of decimal places.

Remember, sometimes you might need to write a zero in the product in order to place the decimal point correctly.

Find: 0.92 × 15.4

Multiply. Write the decimal point in the product.

```
   0.92        2 places
 ×15.4        +1 place
   368
   460
   092
 14.168        3 places
```

Find: 0.49 × 0.05

Multiply. Write the decimal point in the product.

```
    0.49        2 places
 ×  0.05       +2 places
    245
    000
  0.0245        4 places
```
└── Write a zero.

GUIDED PRACTICE

Multiply. Write zeros as needed.

	a	b	c	d
1.	0.5 ×0.8	0.6 ×0.9	5.2 ×0.7	9.6 ×0.4
	0.4 0			
2.	0.6 2 × 0.5	0.1 2 × 0.3	0.0 5 × 0.6	0.1 6 × 0.2
3.	0.4 8 ×6.9 5	0.7 6 ×4 3.5	0.5 6 ×9.1 2	0.2 4 ×1 8.7

Line up the digits. Then find the products. Write zeros as needed.

a

4. $0.137 \times 0.06 =$ _____

```
  0.137
×0.06
```

b

$1.284 \times 0.48 =$ _____

c

$4.507 \times 0.52 =$ _____

PRACTICE

Multiply. Write zeros as needed.

	a	b	c	d
1.	0.4 ×0.8	0.7 ×0.7	1.6 ×0.9	2.5 ×0.8
2.	0.4 8 × 0.3	0.6 4 × 0.5	0.3 1 × 0.4	0.0 9 × 0.6
3.	0.3 5 ×0.1 5	0.8 2 ×0.6 4	0.6 7 ×0.3 9	0.1 7 ×0.7 9
4.	0.1 2 ×3.0 8	0.6 3 ×1 2.6	0.9 9 ×3.8 1	0.4 7 ×6.2 4

Line up the digits. Then find the products. Write zeros as needed.

a
5. $0.95 \times 0.02 =$ _____

b
$3.547 \times 0.68 =$ _____

c
$3.641 \times 0.79 =$ _____

6. $0.15 \times 5.89 =$ _____

$6.5 \times 6.5 =$ _____

$9.47 \times 0.14 =$ _____

MIXED PRACTICE

Find each answer.

	a	b	c	d
1.	3 8.7 +1 6.9	8.0 1 5 −0.9 6 2	$ 1 3.5 5 + 2 6.7 4	$ 3 0.6 8 − 5.9 9

Problem-Solving Strategy: Identify Extra Information

The planet Mercury is 36,000,000 miles from the sun. It orbits, or circles, the sun faster than any other planet. At a speed of 29.76 miles per second, it only takes Mercury 87.969 days to orbit the sun. How far does Mercury travel in 1 minute?

Understand the problem.

- **What do you want to know?**
  how far Mercury travels in 1 minute (60 seconds)

- **What information is given?**
  Mercury's distance from the sun, the miles per second, and the days to complete a full orbit

Plan how to solve it.

- **What strategy can you use?**
  You can identify extra information that is not needed to solve the problem.

Solve it.

- **How can you use this strategy to solve the problem?**
  Reread the problem. Cross out any unnecessary facts. Then you can focus on the needed facts to solve the problem.

  > ~~The planet Mercury is 36,000,000 miles from the sun. It orbits, or circles, the sun faster than any other planet.~~ At a speed of 29.76 miles per second, ~~it only takes Mercury 87.969 days to orbit the sun.~~ How far does Mercury travel in 1 minute?

- **What is the answer?**

  $29.76 \times 60 = 1{,}785.6$

  In 1 minute, Mercury travels 1,785.6 miles.

Look back and check your answer.

- **Is your answer reasonable?**
  You can estimate to check your answer.

  $30 \times 60 = 1{,}800$

  The estimate is close to the answer.
  The answer is reasonable.

In each problem, cross out the extra information. Then solve the problem.

1. Earth is 92.96 million miles from the sun. It orbits the sun in about 365.26 days, traveling at an average speed of 18.51 miles per second. How far does Earth travel in 1 minute? (60 seconds)

Answer _____

2. Fleas can jump up to 150 times the length of their bodies. This is equivalent to a person jumping nearly 1,000 feet. The average flea is about 0.2 inch long. How high can it jump?

Answer _____

3. Fingernails grow about 0.004 inch a day. After not cutting his nails for 44 years, a man in India has the world's longest nails. His thumbnail is 4.67 feet long. How many inches do fingernails grow in 1 week? (7 days)

Answer _____

4. Every day, 274,000 carats of diamonds are mined. One carat is 0.02 grams. The Cullinan Diamond is the largest diamond ever discovered. It is 3,106 carats. How many grams does the Cullinan Diamond weigh?

Answer _____

5. The movie *Forrest Gump* earned a total of $679.7 million worldwide. $329.7 million of that total was made in the United States. *Forrest Gump* was nominated for 13 Academy Awards and won 6. How much of its total earnings were made outside the U.S.?

Answer _____

6. At 179.6 feet, the "Rattler" is the world's tallest wooden roller coaster. Each ride is 2.25 minutes long. "Superman the Escape" is the world's tallest steel roller coaster, at 415 feet. Its ride lasts 0.467 minutes. How much longer is a ride on the "Rattler" than on "Superman"?

Answer _____

Problem-Solving Applications

Solve.

1. A saleswoman receives 32 cents per mile for car expenses. How much does she receive for a 29.5-mile trip? (Hint: Use 0.32 for the cents.)

Answer _____

2. The electricity to run a television costs an average of $0.02 per hour. If you leave the television on for $4\frac{1}{2}$ hours, how much will it cost? (Hint: Change $4\frac{1}{2}$ to a decimal.)

Answer _____

3. Laura earns $7.40 an hour at the bookstore. If she works 12.5 hours this week, how much will she earn?

Answer _____

4. Tim's car averages 15.8 miles for each gallon of gas. How far will his car go on a tankful of gas if the tank holds 16 gallons?

Answer _____

5. Ann paid $17.95 for 100 copies of her newsletter. At this price, how much will 500 copies of the newsletter cost?

Answer _____

6. The speed record for skateboarding is 62.55 miles per hour. How many miles could a skateboarder go in 0.5 hour at this speed?

Answer _____

7. The speed of a boat is measured in knots. One knot is 1.152 miles per hour. The fastest sailboat in the world can travel at a speed of 46.52 knots. How many miles per hour can it sail?

Answer _____

8. A gallon of water weighs 8.355 pounds. A gallon of milk weighs 1.03 times as much as a gallon of water. How much does a gallon of milk weigh? Round your answer to the nearest hundredth.

Answer _____

Dividing by Powers of Ten

To divide a decimal by a power of ten, move the decimal point in the dividend to the left as many places as there are zeros in the divisor.

Remember, sometimes you might need to write zeros in the quotient in order to correctly insert the decimal point.

Study these examples.

$0.75 \div 10 = 0.075$ $0.35 \div 100 = 0.0035$ $0.91 \div 1,000 = 0.00091$

$0.715 \div 10 = 0.0715$ $0.315 \div 100 = 0.00315$ $0.315 \div 1,000 = 0.000315$

$7.5 \div 10 = 0.75$ $3.5 \div 100 = 0.035$ $3.5 \div 1,000 = 0.0035$

$7.05 \div 10 = 0.705$ $3.05 \div 100 = 0.0305$ $3.05 \div 1,000 = 0.00305$

PRACTICE

Divide. Write zeros as needed.

	a	b	c
1.	$6.89 \div 10 =$ _0.689_	$0.7 \div 10 =$ _____	$0.56 \div 10 =$ _____
2.	$12.3 \div 10 =$ _____	$0.49 \div 10 =$ _____	$8.1 \div 10 =$ _____
3.	$14.11 \div 100 =$ _____	$0.03 \div 100 =$ _____	$2.89 \div 100 =$ _____
4.	$37.737 \div 1,000 =$ _____	$9.91 \div 1,000 =$ _____	$134.2 \div 1,000 =$ _____
5.	$0.039 \div 10 =$ _____	$555.5 \div 100 =$ _____	$7.15 \div 1,000 =$ _____

Dividing Decimals by Whole Numbers

To divide a decimal by a whole number, write the decimal point in the quotient directly above the decimal in the dividend. Then divide the same way as you divide whole numbers.

Find: 42.4 ÷ 8

Write a decimal point in the quotient.	Divide.
$8\overline{)42.4}$ (with decimal point above)	$\begin{array}{r} 5.3 \\ 8\overline{)42.4} \\ -40\ \downarrow \\ \hline 24 \\ -24 \\ \hline 0 \end{array}$

Find: $11.88 ÷ 12

Write a decimal point in the quotient.	Divide.
$12\overline{)\$11.88}$ (with decimal point above)	$\begin{array}{r} \$0.99 \\ 12\overline{)\$11.88} \\ -\ 0\ \downarrow \\ \hline 118 \\ -108\ \downarrow \\ \hline 108 \\ -108 \\ \hline 0 \end{array}$

GUIDED PRACTICE

Divide.

	a	b	c	d
1.	$\begin{array}{r} 2.2 \\ 3\overline{)6.6} \\ -6\ \downarrow \\ \hline 0\,6 \\ -0\,6 \\ \hline 0 \end{array}$	$4\overline{)18.4}$	$9\overline{)\$5.76}$	$8\overline{)12.8}$

| **2.** | $22\overline{)26.4}$ | $19\overline{)96.9}$ | $45\overline{)234.0}$ | $25\overline{)\$6.50}$ |

Set up the problems. Then find the quotients.

	a	b	c
3.	37.68 ÷ 60 = _____	543.20 ÷ 10 = _____	31.35 ÷ 57 = _____
	$60\overline{)37.68}$		

PRACTICE

Divide.

	a	*b*	*c*	*d*
1.	3)2 7.9	7)4 5.5	5)1 8.5	9)7 0.2

	a	*b*	*c*	*d*
2.	1 8)6.1 2	3 1)2 2.3 2	5 8)4 3.5	6 5)5 2.6 5

	a	*b*	*c*	*d*
3.	4)$ 1.1 2	6)$ 5 3.8 2	2 7)$ 2 2.9 5	4 2)$ 8 3.5 8

Set up the problems. Then find the quotients.

a	*b*	*c*
4. 25.47 ÷ 3 = _____	63.6 ÷ 12 = _____	38.22 ÷ 49 = _____

MIXED PRACTICE

Find each answer.

	a	*b*	*c*	*d*
1.	2 8 ×4 7	8 9,5 4 3 − 3,5 9 7	5 8,6 3 4 +3 3,0 9 6	8)6,5 1 2

Dividing Decimals by Decimals

To divide a decimal by a decimal, change the divisor to a whole number by moving the decimal point. Move the decimal point in the dividend the same number of places. Then divide.

Remember, write a decimal point in the quotient directly above the position of the *new* decimal point in the dividend.

Find: 8.64 ÷ 0.6

Move each decimal point 1 place.

$$0.6\overline{)8.6\,4}$$

Divide.

```
    1 4.4
6)8 6.4
 -6 ↓
  2 6
 -2 4 ↓
    2 4
   -2 4
      0
```

Find: 0.5280 ÷ 0.96

Move each decimal point 2 places.

$$0.96\overline{)0.5\,2\,8\,0}$$

Divide.

```
    0.5 5
9 6)5 2.8 0
  -4 8 0 ↓
     4 8 0
    -4 8 0
         0
```

GUIDED PRACTICE

Divide.

	a	b	c	d

1.

a.
```
      2.6
3.4)8.8 4
 -6 8 ↓
  2 0 4
 -2 0 4
       0
```

b. $0.9\overline{)1\,5.3}$

c. $0.7\overline{)4.0\,6}$

d. $1.5\overline{)4.9\,5}$

2.

a.
```
       2 1
0.2 3)4.8 3
   -4 6 ↓
     2 3
    -2 3
       0
```

b. $1.9\overline{)5.9\,2\,8}$

c. $0.3\,2\overline{)5.1\,2}$

d. $6.2\overline{)1\,1\,9.6\,6}$

Divide.

	a	b	c	d
1.	0.7)6.5 1	0.5)4.1 5	0.8)2.0 8	0.3)1.6 8
2.	4.2)2.7 3	1.8)7.0 2	2.5)2 4.5	5.7)1 9.3 8
3.	6.1)3 2.9 4	3.9)2 9.6 4	8.4)1 0 5.8 4	7.3)5 7 0.1 3

Set up the problems. Then find the quotients.

a

b

c

4. 6.12 ÷ 3.4 = _____   1.328 ÷ 0.8 = _____   333.32 ÷ 5.2 = _____

Find each answer.

	a	b	c	d
1.	7.9 ×0.6	1 0 0 − 2 6.3 9	2 5.8 +9 7.3 4	4)1 0 2.4

Dividing Whole Numbers by Decimals

To divide a whole number by a decimal, change the divisor
to a whole number by moving the decimal point. To move the
decimal point in the dividend the same number of places, you
will need to add one or more zeros. Then divide.

Find: 48 ÷ 3.2

Move each decimal point 1 place.	Divide.
$3.2\overline{)48.0}$	$\begin{array}{r} 15 \\ 32\overline{)480} \\ -32\downarrow \\ \hline 160 \\ -160 \\ \hline 0 \end{array}$

Find: 39 ÷ 0.13

Move each decimal point 2 places.	Divide.
$0.13\overline{)39.00}$	$\begin{array}{r} 300 \\ 13\overline{)3,900} \\ -39\downarrow \\ \hline 00 \\ -0\downarrow \\ \hline 00 \\ -0 \\ \hline 0 \end{array}$

GUIDED PRACTICE

Divide. Write zeros as needed.

	a	b	c	d
1.	$\begin{array}{r} 4 \\ 0.5\overline{)2.0} \\ -20 \\ \hline 0 \end{array}$	$0.6\overline{)54}$	$1.3\overline{)78}$	$4.5\overline{)675}$
2.	$\begin{array}{r} 200 \\ 0.19\overline{)38.00} \\ -38\downarrow \\ \hline 00 \\ -0\downarrow \\ \hline 00 \\ -0 \\ \hline 0 \end{array}$	$0.50\overline{)425}$	$2.6\overline{)936}$	$9.3\overline{)2,325}$

PRACTICE

Divide. Write zeros as needed.

a	b	c	d
1. $0.2\overline{)6\ 4}$	$0.9\overline{)7\ 2}$	$0.4\overline{)7\ 6}$	$0.7\overline{)1\ 7\ 5}$
2. $4.1\overline{)3\ 2\ 8}$	$6.7\overline{)4\ 0\ 2}$	$2.9\overline{)5\ 2\ 2}$	$8.3\overline{)4,0\ 6\ 7}$
3. $0.14\overline{)8\ 4}$	$0.36\overline{)9\ 7\ 2}$	$0.99\overline{)3,4\ 6\ 5}$	$7.2\overline{)1\ 3,1\ 7\ 6}$

Set up the problems. Then find the quotients.

a	b	c
4. $288 \div 0.8 =$ _____	$636 \div 1.2 =$ _____	$4,698 \div 0.54 =$ _____

MIXED PRACTICE

Compare. Write <, >, or =.

a	b	c
1. 1.7 _____ 0.7	0.359 _____ 0.36	5.94 _____ 59.4

Write in order from least to greatest.

a	b
2. 6.7 6.07 0.67 _____	0.68 0.86 0.08 _____

Decimal Quotients

Often when you divide, your answer will have a remainder.
You can add zeros in the dividend and continue to divide until
the remainder is zero. If the dividend is a whole number, add a
decimal point and add zeros as needed.

Remember, zeros also may be needed in the quotient.

Find: 26.7 ÷ 4

Divide until you have a remainder.	Add zeros.
$$\begin{array}{r} 6.6 \\ 4\overline{)2\,6.7} \\ -2\,4\downarrow \\ \hline 2\,7 \\ -2\,4 \\ \hline 3 \end{array}$$	$$\begin{array}{r} 6.6\,7\,5 \\ 4\overline{)2\,6.7\,0\,0} \\ -2\,4\downarrow \\ \hline 2\,7 \\ -2\,4\downarrow \\ \hline 3\,0 \\ -2\,8\downarrow \\ \hline 2\,0 \\ -2\,0 \\ \hline 0 \end{array}$$

Find: 802 ÷ 4

Divide until you have a remainder	Add a decimal point and a zero.
$$\begin{array}{r} 2\,0\,0 \\ 4\overline{)8\,0\,2} \\ -8\downarrow \\ \hline 0\,0 \\ -\,0 \\ \hline 0\,2 \end{array}$$	$$\begin{array}{r} 2\,0\,0.5 \\ 4\overline{)8\,0\,2.0} \\ -8\downarrow \\ \hline 0\,0 \\ -\,0 \\ \hline 0\,2 \\ -\,0 \\ \hline 2\,0 \\ -2\,0 \\ \hline 0 \end{array}$$

PRACTICE

Divide. Write zeros as needed.

a	b	c	d

1.
$$\begin{array}{r} 2.0\,7\,5 \\ 4\overline{)8.3\,0\,0} \\ -8\downarrow \\ \hline 0\,3 \\ -\,0\downarrow \\ \hline 3\,0 \\ -2\,8\downarrow \\ \hline 2\,0 \\ -2\,0 \\ \hline 0 \end{array}$$
   $5\overline{)5\,7.1}$ $9\overline{)1\,8.6\,3}$ $6\overline{)0.6\,5\,7\,0}$

2.
$$\begin{array}{r} 1.7\,5 \\ 3\,2\overline{)5\,6.0\,0} \\ -3\,2\downarrow \\ \hline 2\,4\,0 \\ -2\,2\,4\downarrow \\ \hline 1\,6\,0 \\ -1\,6\,0 \\ \hline 0 \end{array}$$
   $4\,0\overline{)8\,5\,0}$ $1\,8\overline{)4\,5}$ $8\,5\overline{)8,7\,0\,4}$

Rounding Quotients

Sometimes when you have a remainder, adding zeros to the dividend and continuing to divide will result in a remainder of zero. Sometimes the remainder will never be zero, or may take too many steps. You may need to round the quotient. You may also need to round the quotient when you are dividing money.

Find: 23 ÷ 7.1

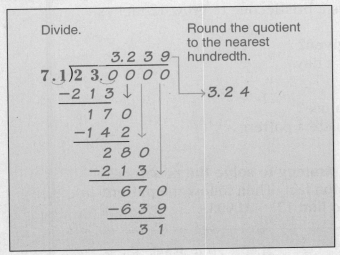

Find: $1.85 ÷ 10

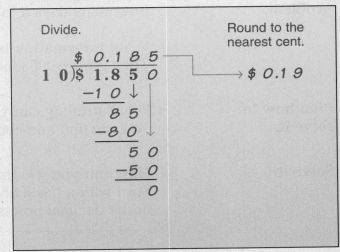

PRACTICE

Divide. Round to the place named.

a	b	c
nearest tenth	nearest hundredth	nearest tenth

1.
$$\begin{array}{r} 6.27 \rightarrow 6.3 \\ 5.1\overline{)3\,2.0\,0\,0} \\ -3\,0\,6 \downarrow \\ 1\,4\,0 \\ -1\,0\,2 \downarrow \\ 3\,8\,0 \\ -3\,5\,7 \\ 2\,3 \end{array}$$

$3\overline{)2\,2}$

$8\overline{)6.4\,8}$

nearest cent	nearest cent	nearest dollar

2.
$$\begin{array}{r} \$0.3\,2\,5 \rightarrow \$0.3\,3 \\ 6\overline{)\$1.9\,5\,0} \\ -1\,8 \downarrow \\ 1\,5 \\ -1\,2 \downarrow \\ 3\,0 \end{array}$$

$10\overline{)\$4\,0\,5.7\,5}$

$29\overline{)\$6\,0\,8}$

Problem-Solving Strategy: Complete a Pattern

Earth's oldest living organisms are bristlecone pine trees. One found in California is almost 5,000 years old. Bristlecones are also one of Earth's slowest growers, at only 0.0003 inch a day. How many days does it take the tree to grow 12 inches (1 foot)?

Understand the problem.

- **What do you want to know?**
  how many days it takes a bristlecone to grow 12 inches

- **What information is given?**
  They grow 0.0003 inch a day.

Plan how to solve it.

- **What strategy can you use?**
  You can find and complete a pattern.

Solve it.

- **How can you use this strategy to solve the problem?**
  Start with a basic division fact. Then follow the pattern in the decimal points to find $12 \div 0.0003$.

12	÷	3	=	4	← Basic Fact
12	÷	0.3	=	40	
12	÷	0.03	=	400	
12	÷	0.003	=	4,000	
12	÷	0.0003	=	40,000	

Decimal point moves **4 places to the left.** Decimal point moves **4 places to the right.**

- **What is the answer?**
  It takes 40,000 days for a bristlecone pine tree to grow 12 inches.

Look back and check your answer.

- **Is your answer reasonable?**
  You can check your division with multiplication.

$$
\begin{array}{r}
40,000 \\
\times\ 0.0003 \\
\hline
12.0000
\end{array}
$$

The product matches the dividend.
The answer is reasonable.

Complete a pattern to solve each problem.

1. Human hair grows about 0.02 inch a day. How many days does it take hair to grow 6 inches?

   6 ÷ 2 = ___3___

   6 ÷ 0.2 = ___30___

   6 ÷ 0.02 = _____

   Answer _____

2. A garden snail moves only 0.03 miles per hour. How far can a snail move in 8 hours?

   8 × 3 = ___24___

   8 × 0.3 = ___2.4___

   8 × 0.03 = _____

   Answer _____

3. One milliliter is equal to 0.001 of a liter. How many milliliters are in a 2-liter bottle of soda?

   2 ÷ 1 = _____

   2 ÷ 0.1 = _____

   2 ÷ 0.01 = _____

   2 ÷ 0.001 = _____

   Answer _____

4. In a certain week, one Japanese yen was worth 0.008 United States dollars. How many United States dollars could you get for 10 yen?

   10 × 8 = _____

   10 × 0.8 = _____

   10 × 0.08 = _____

   10 × 0.008 = _____

   Answer _____

5. One nickel is worth 0.05 of a dollar. How many nickels do you need to have $15.00?

   15 ÷ 5 = _____

   15 ÷ 0.5 = _____

   15 ÷ 0.05 = _____

   Answer _____

6. In some places, sales tax is 0.05 times the price of an item. If a hat costs $9.00, how much sales tax will be charged?

   9 × 5 = _____

   9 × 0.5 = _____

   9 × 0.05 = _____

   Answer _____

Problem-Solving Applications

Solve.

1. Lee's farm is 369.2 acres. If the farm is divided into 4 equal plots, how many acres will each plot be?

Answer _____

2. Electricity is measured in watts. One kilowatt is 1,000 watts. How many kilowatts are in 2,674 watts?

Answer _____

3. On one trip, Brenda drove 1,192.39 miles and used a total of 47 gallons of gas. How many miles per gallon did her car average?

Answer _____

4. Cat food is on sale for $2.79 for 4 cans. Steve only wants to buy 1 can. How much will it cost? Round this price to the nearest tenth of a cent.

Answer _____

5. Alicia jogged 8.5 miles in 2.5 hours. What was her average distance per hour?

Answer _____

6. Malcolm earned $48.18 for 5.5 hours of work. What was his hourly rate of pay?

Answer _____

7. The rainfall for the last 3 months was 5.60 inches, 6.15 inches, and 4.3 inches. What was the average monthly rainfall? (Hint: Add the 3 amounts and divide by 3.)

Answer _____

8. The check for dinner was $96.00. The 4 friends added a tip (0.15 times the total check). If they split the final total evenly, how much did they each pay?

Answer _____

Multiply. Write zeros as needed.

a	*b*	*c*
1. $2.31 \times 10 =$ _____	$0.56 \times 100 =$ _____	$7.8 \times 1{,}000 =$ _____
2. $0.83 \times 10 =$ _____	$6.4 \times 100 =$ _____	$0.38 \times 1{,}000 =$ _____

Multiply. Write zeros as needed.

a	*b*	*c*	*d*
3. $\begin{array}{r} 7.2\,3 \\ \times\quad 2 \\ \hline \end{array}$	$\begin{array}{r} 6 \\ \times 5.0\,1\,4 \\ \hline \end{array}$	$\begin{array}{r} \$\,0.6\,7 \\ \times\quad\quad 3 \\ \hline \end{array}$	$\begin{array}{r} 8 \\ \times 0.9\,1 \\ \hline \end{array}$
4. $\begin{array}{r} 6\,8 \\ \times\quad 0.0\,5 \\ \hline \end{array}$	$\begin{array}{r} 5\,7\,4 \\ \times\quad 3.7 \\ \hline \end{array}$	$\begin{array}{r} 0.9\,3\,1 \\ \times\quad\quad 7\,5 \\ \hline \end{array}$	$\begin{array}{r} \$\,1\,6.9\,9 \\ \times\quad\quad 1\,2 \\ \hline \end{array}$
5. $\begin{array}{r} 0.9 \\ \times 0.5 \\ \hline \end{array}$	$\begin{array}{r} 3.6 \\ \times 0.7 \\ \hline \end{array}$	$\begin{array}{r} 1.6 \\ \times 8.4 \\ \hline \end{array}$	$\begin{array}{r} 1\,2.7 \\ \times\quad 6.3 \\ \hline \end{array}$
6. $\begin{array}{r} 4.2\,7 \\ \times 0.0\,2 \\ \hline \end{array}$	$\begin{array}{r} 0.0\,5\,5 \\ \times\quad 1.0\,8 \\ \hline \end{array}$	$\begin{array}{r} 6.\,7 \\ \times 9.3 \\ \hline \end{array}$	$\begin{array}{r} 0.9\,3\,1 \\ \times\quad\quad 5.8 \\ \hline \end{array}$

Line up the digits. Then find the products. Write zeros as needed.

a	*b*	*c*
7. $17 \times 2.5 =$ _____	$25 \times 7.3 =$ _____	$32 \times 41.5 =$ _____
8. $0.63 \times 0.5 =$ _____	$0.29 \times 1.84 =$ _____	$3.18 \times 1.54 =$ _____

Divide. Write zeros as needed.

a	*b*	*c*

9. $0.34 \div 10 =$ _____ $0.92 \div 100 =$ _____ $1.58 \div 1{,}000 =$ _____

10. $0.05 \div 10 =$ _____ $1.9 \div 100 =$ _____ $6.495 \div 1{,}000 =$ _____

Divide.

a	*b*	*c*	*d*

11.

$7\overline{)9.1}$ $5\overline{)3\ 1.5}$ $4\overline{)\$\ 3\ 0.4\ 0}$ $8\overline{)1\ 6.8}$

12.

$2.6\overline{)3.9}$ $0.9\overline{)1\ 9.8}$ $0.1\ 6\overline{)3.0\ 4}$ $8.2\overline{)2\ 1\ 7.3}$

13.

$5.6\overline{)1{,}6\ 8\ 0}$ $0.8\overline{)1\ 6}$ $2.5\overline{)2{,}8\ 2\ 0}$ $3.4\overline{)1{,}5\ 9\ 8}$

Divide. Round to the place named.

a	*b*	*c*
nearest tenth	nearest cent	nearest hundredth

14.

$2.3\overline{)2.8\ 7\ 5}$ $7\overline{)\$\ 1\ 5.0\ 2}$ $5\overline{)1.7\ 3\ 2}$

In each problem, cross out the extra information. Then solve the problem.

15. Pluto is the farthest planet from the sun, at 5.9 billion kilometers. It takes Pluto 90.950 days to orbit the sun at a speed of 4.74 kilometers per second. How far does Pluto travel in 30 seconds?

Answer _____

16. In one year, 31.9% of students in the United States had access to a computer. The average student that year used a computer 5.3 hours a week. How many hours did the average student use a computer each day? Round the answer to the nearest tenth. (1 week = 7 days)

Answer _____

17. In-line skates were introduced to the United States in the late 1970s. In 1998, the record for the highest speed on in-line skates was set at 64.02 miles per hour. How far could a person skate in 2 hours at this speed?

Answer _____

18. On December 17, 1903, Orville Wright became the first man to fly an engine-powered airplane. His flight took place near Kitty Hawk, North Carolina, and covered 120 feet in 0.2 minutes. On average, how many feet per minute did the plane fly?

Answer _____

Find and complete a pattern to solve each problem.

19. One cup is about 0.06 of a gallon. How many cups of water do you need to fill a 54-gallon fish tank?

$54 \div 6 =$ _____

$54 \div 0.6 =$ _____

$54 \div 0.06 =$ _____

Answer _____

20. A lamp with one bulb costs an average of $0.02 per hour for electricity. If you leave a lamp turned on for 12 hours, how much will it cost?

$12 \times 2 =$ _____

$12 \times 0.2 =$ _____

$12 \times 0.02 =$ _____

Answer _____

Customary Length

The customary units that are used to measure length are **inch, foot, yard,** and **mile.** The chart gives the relationship of one unit to another.

You can multiply or divide to change units of measurement.

To compare two measurements, first change them to the same unit.

1 foot (ft)	=	12 inches (in.)
1 yard (yd)	=	3 ft
	=	36 in.
1 mile (mi)	=	1,760 yd
	=	5,280 ft

Find: $3\frac{1}{2}$ ft = _____ in.

To change larger units to smaller units, multiply.

1 ft = 12 in.

$3\frac{1}{2} \times 12 = \frac{7}{2} \times 12 = 42$

$3\frac{1}{2}$ ft = 42 in.

Find: 10 ft = _____ yd

To change smaller units to larger units, divide.

3 ft = 1 yd

$10 \div 3 = 3\frac{1}{3}$

10 ft = $3\frac{1}{3}$ yd

PRACTICE

Change each measurement to the smaller unit.

	a	b	c
1.	$5\frac{1}{6}$ yd = _____ ft	$1\frac{1}{2}$ mi = _____ ft	$7\frac{1}{3}$ ft = _____ in.
2.	$1\frac{1}{4}$ yd = _____ in.	21 yd = _____ ft	4 mi = _____ yd

Change each measurement to the larger unit.

	a	b	c
3.	51 in. = _____ ft	38 ft = _____ yd	60 in. = _____ ft
4.	4,400 yd = _____ mi	222 in. = _____ ft	15,840 ft = _____ mi

Compare. Write <, >, or =.

	a	b
5.	24 in. ____<____ 4 ft	3 mi _____ 10,000 ft

1 ft = 12 in.
4 ft = 4 × 12 = 48 in.

	a	b
6.	12 ft _____ 4 yd	3,600 yd _____ 2 mi

Customary Weight

The customary units that are used to measure weight are **ounce, pound,** and **ton.** The chart shows the relationship of one unit to another.

1 pound (lb) = 16 ounces (oz)	
1 ton (T) = 2,000 pounds	

Find: $5\frac{1}{2}$ lb = _____ oz

To change larger units to smaller units, multiply.

$$1 \text{ lb} = 16 \text{ oz}$$
$$5\frac{1}{2} \times 16 = \frac{11}{2} \times 16 = 88$$
$$5\frac{1}{2} \text{ lb} = 88 \text{ oz}$$

Find: 6,500 lb = _____ T

To change smaller units to larger units, divide.

$$2,000 \text{ lb} = 1 \text{ T}$$
$$6,500 \div 2,000 = 3\frac{1}{4}$$
$$6,500 \text{ lb} = 3\frac{1}{4} \text{ T}$$

PRACTICE

Change each measurement to the smaller unit.

a	b	c
1. $3\frac{1}{4}$ lb = _____ oz	$2\frac{1}{2}$ T = _____ lb	6 lb = _____ oz
2. 4 T = _____ lb	$1\frac{3}{8}$ lb = _____ oz	$4\frac{3}{16}$ lb = _____ oz

Change each measurement to the larger unit.

a	b	c
3. 53 oz = _____ lb	7,000 lb = _____ T	80 oz = _____ lb
4. 72 oz = _____ lb	36 oz = _____ lb	2,400 lb = _____ T

Compare. Write <, >, or =.

a	b
5. 40 lb ___=___ 640 oz	10,000 lb _____ 4 T
$1 \text{ lb} = 16 \text{ oz}$	
$40 \text{ lb} = 40 \times 16 = 640 \text{ oz}$	
6. 3.2 T _____ 6,000 lb	80.7 oz _____ 5.3 lb
7. $6\frac{1}{2}$ lb _____ 100 oz	$\frac{1}{8}$ T _____ 300 lb

Customary Capacity

The customary units that are used to measure **capacity** are **cup, pint, quart,** and **gallon.** The chart shows the relationship of one unit to another.

1 pint (pt)	= 2 cups (c)
1 quart (qt)	= 2 pt
	= 4 c
1 gallon (gal)	= 4 qt
	= 8 pt
	= 16 c

Find: $3\frac{3}{4}$ **qt =** _____ **c**

> To change larger units to smaller units, multiply.
>
> $$1 \text{ qt} = 4 \text{ c}$$
> $$3\frac{3}{4} \times 4 = \frac{15}{4} \times 4 = 15$$
> $$3\frac{3}{4} \text{ qt} = 15 \text{ c}$$

Find: **21 qt =** _____ **gal**

> To change smaller units to larger units, divide.
>
> $$4 \text{ qt} = 1 \text{ gal}$$
> $$21 \div 4 = 5\frac{1}{4}$$
> $$21 \text{ qt} = 5\frac{1}{4} \text{ gal}$$

PRACTICE

Change each measurement to the smaller unit.

	a	*b*	*c*
1.	$8\frac{1}{2}$ pt = _____ c	$2\frac{1}{4}$ gal = _____ qt	13 qt = _____ pt
2.	$4\frac{1}{8}$ gal = _____ pt	9 qt = _____ c	$1\frac{1}{2}$ gal = _____ c

Change each measurement to the larger unit.

	a	*b*	*c*
3.	7 c = _____ qt	21 pt = _____ gal	11 c = _____ pt
4.	24 qt = _____ gal	14 pt = _____ qt	54 c = _____ gal

Compare. Write <, >, or =.

a

5. 12 c _____ > _____ 5 pt
1 pt = 2 c
5 pt = 5 × 2 = 10 c

b

50 gal _____ 2,000 qt

6. $5\frac{1}{2}$ qt _____ 22 c

15.6 pt _____ 2 gal

Computing Measures

You can add, subtract, multiply, and divide measures that are given in two units. For example, 1 yd 5 in. uses 2 units to measure one length.

Find: 1 lb 14 oz + 6 lb 10 oz

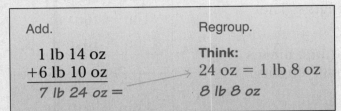

Add.	Regroup.
1 lb 14 oz +6 lb 10 oz 7 lb 24 oz =	**Think:** 24 oz = 1 lb 8 oz 8 lb 8 oz

Find: 5 × 4 gal 3 qt

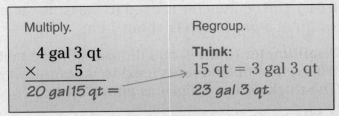

Multiply.	Regroup.
4 gal 3 qt × 5 20 gal 15 qt =	**Think:** 15 qt = 3 gal 3 qt 23 gal 3 qt

Find: 12 ft 4 in. − 6 ft 9 in.

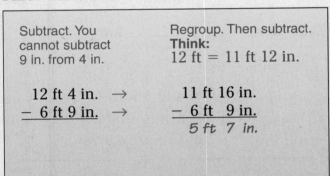

Subtract. You cannot subtract 9 in. from 4 in.	Regroup. Then subtract. **Think:** 12 ft = 11 ft 12 in.
12 ft 4 in. → − 6 ft 9 in. →	11 ft 16 in. − 6 ft 9 in. 5 ft 7 in.

Find: 8 T 200 lb ÷ 6

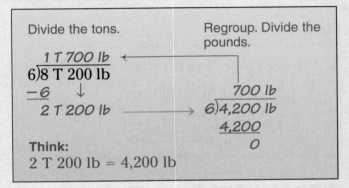

Divide the tons.

$$6\overline{)8\ T\ 200\ lb}$$

1 T 700 lb ← ... Regroup. Divide the pounds.

−6 ↓
2 T 200 lb

Think:
2 T 200 lb = 4,200 lb

$$6\overline{)4{,}200\ lb}$$ 700 lb, 4,200, 0

PRACTICE

Find each answer.

	a	b	c
1.	5 gal 2 qt +2 gal 3 qt 7 gal 5 qt = 8 gal 1 qt	9 ft 6 in. +4 ft 8 in.	7 yd 1 ft +3 yd 2 ft
2.	8 yd 1 ft −6 yd 2 ft	5 gal 2 qt −3 gal 3 qt	24 lb 8 oz −10 lb 12 oz
3.	18 lb 6 oz × 4	5 ft 8 in. × 7	6 T 500 lb × 8
4.	3)5 gal 1 qt	8)10 lb 8 oz	7)9 yd 1 ft

Metric Length

The **meter** (m) is the basic metric unit of length. A meter can be measured with a meter stick. The length of your arm is about 0.7 m.

A **centimeter** (cm) is one hundredth of a meter. (*Centi* means 0.01.) The centimeter is used to measure small lengths. The width of a paper clip is about 1 cm.

A **millimeter** (mm) is one thousandth of a meter. (*Milli* means 0.001.) The millimeter is used to measure very small lengths. The thickness of a nickel is about 2 mm.

A **kilometer** (km) is one thousand meters. (*Kilo* means 1,000.) The kilometer is used to measure long distances. The distance between two cities can be measured in kilometers.

⊢———⌒⌐ 1 cm
⋈ ⌒ 1 mm

| 1 km = 1,000 m |
| 1 m = 100 cm |
| 1 cm = 10 mm |

| 1 m = 0.001 km |
| 1 cm = 0.01 m |
| 1 mm = 0.1 cm |

Find: 8.2 m = _____ cm

To change larger units to smaller units, multiply.

1 m = 100 cm

8.2 × 100 = 820

8.2 m = 820 cm

Find: 63 m = _____ km

To change smaller units to larger units, divide.

1,000 m = 1 km

63 ÷ 1,000 = 0.063

63 m = 0.063 km

PRACTICE

Circle the best measurement.

      a

1. length of a snail

   2 cm   2 m

                           b

distance from Boston to New York

300 m   300 km

2. width of a paper clip

   8 mm   8 cm

length of a car

5 cm   5 m

Change each measurement to the smaller unit.

	a	*b*	*c*
3.	14.5 km = _____ m	7.25 m = _____ cm	18 cm = _____ mm
4.	3.4 m = _____ cm	21 m = _____ mm	0.9 km = _____ m

Change each measurement to the larger unit.

	a	*b*	*c*
5.	48 mm = _____ cm	79.6 cm = _____ m	61 m = _____ km
6.	8,542 m = _____ km	3,128 mm = _____ m	930 cm = _____ m

Metric Mass

The word **mass** is not often used outside the field of science. The common term for mass is weight.

The **gram** (g) is the basic unit of mass. The gram is used to measure the weight of very light objects. A dime weighs about 2 grams.

The **kilogram** (kg) is one thousand grams. It is used to measure the weight of heavier objects. Use kg for the weight of a bicycle. Remember, *kilo* means 1,000.

1 kg = 1,000 g
1 g = 0.001 kg

Find: 8.4 kg = _____ g

To change larger units to smaller units, multiply.

$$1 \text{ kg} = 1,000 \text{ g}$$
$$8.4 \times 1,000 = 8,400$$
$$8.4 \text{ kg} = 8,400 \text{ g}$$

Find: 24.7 g = _____ kg

To change smaller units to larger units, divide.

$$1,000 \text{ g} = 1 \text{ kg}$$
$$24.7 \div 1,000 = 0.0247$$
$$24.7 \text{ g} = 0.0247 \text{ kg}$$

PRACTICE

Circle the best measurement.

 a   b

1. weight of a large dog

   27 g   27 kg

   weight of a package of frozen vegetables

   283 g   28.3 kg

2. weight of a bagel

   70 g   7 kg

   weight of a television

   450 g   45 kg

Change each measurement to the smaller unit.

 a   b   c

3. 32 kg = _____ g   0.007 kg = _____ g   1.8 kg = _____ g

4. 0.49 kg = _____ g   825 kg = _____ g   6.783 kg = _____ g

Change each measurement to the larger unit.

 a   b   c

5. 12.8 g = _____ kg   9 g = _____ kg   137 g = _____ kg

6. 5,268 g = _____ kg   25 g = _____ kg   4.9 g = _____ kg

Metric Capacity

The **liter** (L) is the basic metric unit of capacity. A liter of liquid will fill a box 10 centimeters on each side. A large jug of apple cider holds about 4 L.

A **milliliter** (mL) is one thousandth of a liter. It is used to measure very small amounts of liquid. A milliliter of liquid will fill a box 1 centimeter on each side. A small carton of milk holds about 250 mL.

Remember, *milli* means 0.001.

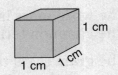

1 L = 1,000 mL
1 mL = 0.001 L

Find: 2.5 L = _____ mL

To change larger units to smaller units, multiply.
1 L = 1,000 mL
2.5 × 1,000 = 2,500
2.5 L = 2,500 mL

Find: 5,672 mL = _____ L

To change smaller units to larger units, divide.
1,000 mL = 1 L
5,672 ÷ 1,000 = 5.672
5,672 mL = 5.672 L

PRACTICE

Circle the best measurement.

　　　　　　　　　　　　a　　　　　　　　　　　　　　　　　　　　*b*

1. capacity of a container of yogurt　　　capacity of a can of tomato juice
　　200 mL　　　200 L　　　　　　　　　　450 mL　　　450 L

2. capacity of a bathtub　　　　　　　　　capacity of a large carton of juice
　　50 mL　　　50 L　　　　　　　　　　　2.84 mL　　　2.84 L

Change each measurement to the smaller unit.

　　　　　a　　　　　　　　　　　　　*b*　　　　　　　　　　　　　*c*

3. 27 L = _____ mL　　　5.3 L = _____ mL　　　7.45 L = _____ mL

4. 0.825 L = _____ mL　　2 L = _____ mL　　　39.6 L = _____ mL

Change each measurement to the larger unit.

　　　　　a　　　　　　　　　　　　　*b*　　　　　　　　　　　　　*c*

5. 3,096 mL = _____ L　　6,000 mL = _____ L　　412.5 mL = _____ L

6. 58 mL = _____ L　　　798 mL = _____ L　　　19.2 mL = _____ L

Computing Metric Measures

You can add, subtract, multiply, and divide measures that are given in two units. For example, 2 m 26 cm uses 2 units to measure one length.

Find: 2 km 750 m + 1 km 300 m

Add.	Regroup.
2 km 750 m +1 km 300 m ‾‾‾‾‾‾‾‾‾‾ 3 km 1,050 m =	**Think:** 1,050 m = 1 km 50 m *4 km 50 m*

Find: 3 × 2 L 425 mL

Multiply.	Regroup.
2 L 425 mL × 3 ‾‾‾‾‾‾‾‾‾ 6 L 1,275 mL =	**Think:** 1,275 mL = 1 L 275 mL *7 L 275 mL*

Find: 4 kg 200 g − 1 kg 900 g

Subtract. You cannot subtract 900 g from 200 g.	Regroup. Then subtract.

4 kg 200 g →
−1 kg 900 g →
	Think:
	4 kg = 3 kg 1,000 g
	
	  3 kg 1,200 g
	−1 kg 900 g
	‾‾‾‾‾‾‾‾‾‾‾
	  2 kg 300 g

Find: 6 L 500 mL ÷ 5

Divide the liters.	Regroup. Divide the milliliters.

1 L 300 mL
5)‾6 L 500 mL
−5   ↓
‾‾‾‾‾
  1 L 500 mL →
 	
Think:
1 L 500 mL = 1,500 mL
	300 mL
	5)‾1,500 mL
	  1,500
	‾‾‾‾‾
	    0

PRACTICE

Find each answer. Simplify.

	a	b	c
1.	19 cm 2 mm +15 cm 29 mm ‾‾‾‾‾‾‾‾‾‾‾ *34 cm 31 mm = 37 cm 1 mm*	3 kg 750 g +4 kg 375 g	8 L 125 mL +3 L 650 mL
2.	8 kg 150 g −6 kg 200 g	5 L 425 mL −2 L 300 mL	33 m 65 cm −10 m 70 cm
3.	9 km 375 m × 3	5 kg 30 g × 7	7 L 750 mL × 6
4.	4)‾5 kg 100 g	5)‾19 L 200 mL	2)‾4 km 500 m

Problem-Solving Strategy:
Make an Organized List

Every metric measurement has a **prefix** and a **base unit.** The prefix *deca* means 10. The prefix *mega* means 1,000,000. A *deca*gon is a polygon with 10 sides, and a *mega*ton is 1,000,000 tons. How many different metric measurements can you write with these two prefixes and the base units meter, liter, and gram?

Understand the problem.

- **What do you want to know?**
  how many different metric measurements you can write with those prefixes and base units

- **What information is given?**
  Prefixes: deca and mega
  Base Units: meter, liter, and gram

Plan how to solve it.

- **What strategy can you use?**
  You can make a list of the different prefix–base unit combinations. Then count the combinations.

Solve it.

- **How can you use this strategy to solve the problem?**
  Start with the first prefix and list all of its bases.
  Then do the same thing for the other prefix.

Prefix	Base	Measurement
deca-	meter	decameter
	liter	decaliter
	gram	decagram
mega-	meter	megameter
	liter	megaliter
	gram	megagram

- **What is the answer?**
  You can write 6 different metric measurements.

Look back and check your answer.

- **Is your answer reasonable?**
  You can multiply to check your answer.

  number of prefixes $\times$ number of bases = number of combinations

  $2 \times 3 = 6$

  The product matches the count.
  The answer is reasonable.

Make an organized list to solve each problem.

1. The prefix *hecto* means 100. The prefix *deci* means $\frac{1}{10}$. What are the possible measurements with these prefixes and the base units meter and gram?

Answer _____

_____

_____

_____

2. The sports banquet gave a choice of meat or fish. Each person could choose two of three kinds of vegetables, potatoes, peas, or carrots, and one of two desserts, cake or pie. How many different meal choices are there?

Answer _____

_____

_____

3. Sam, Tim, and Chantall all want to sit next to each other at the movies. In how many different ways can they do this?

Answer _____

4. There are three main trails at the park. One is 1.2 km, one is 2.5 km, and the third is 4 km long. You can hike, bike, or ride a horse. How many different ways can you explore the trails?

Answer _____

Problem-Solving Applications

Solve.

1. The trip from Baltimore to Washington D.C., is $36\frac{4}{5}$ miles. Lucy makes 5 round trips a week. How far does she travel during one week?

   Answer _____

2. The roast weighed $5\frac{1}{4}$ pounds. Andrea cut it into three equal pieces. How much did each piece weigh?

   Answer _____

3. Mark bought a 96-ounce container of milk. How many 6-ounce servings are in the container?

   Answer _____

4. The juice from one orange measures about one-half cup. How many oranges does it take to fill 6 cups with juice?

   Answer _____

5. Ted weighs 33.5 kilograms. His brother weighs twice as much. How much does Ted's brother weigh?

   Answer _____

6. Nick rode his bicycle 0.3 kilometers in 3 minutes. At this same rate, how many minutes would it take him to ride one kilometer?

   Answer _____

7. George needs 1 gallon of paint. One quart costs $3.99 and one gallon costs $16.49. What is the least expensive way for George to buy the 1 gallon?

   Answer _____

8. Tyler's fish tank holds 25 gallons. He added 4 gallons 1 quart to fill the tank. How much water was in the tank before Tyler added more?

   Answer _____

Change each measurement to the smaller unit.

	a	b	c

1. $4\frac{1}{3}$ yd = _____ ft $2\frac{1}{4}$ mi = _____ yd $2\frac{1}{6}$ yd = _____ in.

2. $1\frac{1}{5}$ T = _____ lb   7 lb = _____ oz $2\frac{1}{2}$ lb = _____ oz

3. $5\frac{1}{4}$ gal = _____ pt $2\frac{1}{2}$ pt = _____ c   7 qt = _____ c

4. 13.5 km = _____ m   21 cm = _____ mm $4\frac{1}{2}$ m = _____ cm

5. 3 kg = _____ g $4\frac{1}{2}$ kg = _____ g $3\frac{1}{5}$ kg = _____ g

6. $1\frac{1}{4}$ L = _____ mL   21 L = _____ mL   4 L = _____ mL

Change each measurement to the larger unit.

	a	b	c

7. 78 in. = _____ ft   3,520 yd = _____ mi   22 ft = _____ yd

8. 80 oz = _____ lb   4,000 lb = _____ T   168 oz = _____ lb

9. 11 pt = _____ qt   56 c = _____ gal   7 qt = _____ gal

10. 830 cm = _____ m   75 mm = _____ cm   1,123 m = _____ km

11. 5.9 g = _____ kg   112 g = _____ kg   2,102 g = _____ kg

12. 2,500 mL = _____ L   21.5 mL = _____ L   425 mL = _____ L

Circle the best measurement.

a

13. distance from Miami to Atlanta

30 m   300 km

b

length of a desk

2.5 m   250 mm

14. weight of a pencil

2 kg   2 g

weight of a school bus

30 g   3,000 kg

15. capacity of a bottle

3 L   3 mL

capacity of a carton of apple juice

230 mL   2.3 L

Compare. Write <, >, or =.

a

16. 36 in. _____ 4 ft

b

3 km _____ 30,000 m

17. 128 oz _____ 10 lb

12 gal _____ 40 c

18. 6.2 L _____ 62,000 mL

5,000 g _____ 4 kg

Find each answer.

a

19. 2 mi 3 ft
     +1 mi 5 ft

b

 3 L 6 mL
+2 L 2 mL

c

 7 lb 5 oz
+4 lb 2 oz

20. 7 gal 3 qt
     −4 gal 2 qt

 2 kg 300 g
−1 kg 200 g

 14 ft 8 in.
− 9 ft 11 in.

21. 3 km 2 m
     ×   5

 8 T 62 lb
×   2

 16 gal 5 pt
×   6

22.

4)12 lb 5 oz

3)5 cm 7 mm

2)6 ft 10 in.

Make an organized list to solve each problem.

23. Lucky's Market sells milk in three sizes of containers: 1 gallon, 1 pint, or 1 quart. The market has skim and whole milk. How many different milk choices are sold in Lucky's Market?

Answer _____

24. Sam packed black pants, jeans, and khaki pants for his vacation. He packed three different T-shirts: blue, white, and black. How many different outfits can he wear?

Answer _____

25. Matt has $0.75 in United States coins. He has exactly 1 half-dollar and no pennies. What are all the possible coin combinations Matt could have?

Answer _____

26. There are four marbles in a bag. One is black, one is silver, one is clear, and one is blue. You reach inside without looking and choose 2 marbles. What are all the possible marble pairs you could pick?

Answer _____

Points, Lines, and Planes

A **point** is an exact location in space.

A **plane** is a flat surface that extends forever in all directions. It is named by any three points.

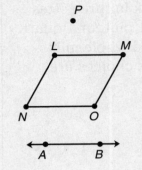

point *P* or *P*

plane *LMN*

A **line** is an endless straight path.

line *AB* or line *BA*

$\overleftrightarrow{AB}$ or $\overleftrightarrow{BA}$

A **line segment** is a straight path between two points.

line segment *RS* or line segment *SR*

$\overline{RS}$ or $\overline{SR}$

A **ray** is an endless straight path starting at one point.

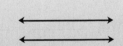

ray *BG*

$\overrightarrow{BG}$

Within a plane, lines can have different relationships.

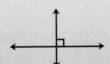

Lines that cross at one point are **intersecting lines.**

Lines that intersect to form four 90° angles are **perpendicular lines.**

Lines that never intersect are **parallel lines.** They are always the same distance apart.

GUIDED PRACTICE

Use the drawing at right for Exercises 1–8.

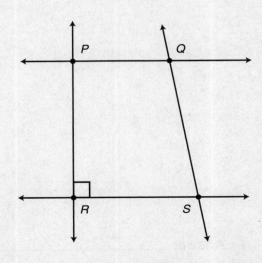

1. Name a plane. _____ *plane PQR* _____

2. Name a line. _____

3. Name a line segment. _____

4. Name a ray. _____

5. Name a point. _____

6. Name 2 parallel lines. _____

7. Name 2 intersecting lines. _____

8. Name 2 perpendicular lines. _____

PRACTICE

Name each figure. Write *point, plane, line, line segment,* or *ray.*

         a   *b*   *c*   *d*

1.

       __line__

Name each figure using symbols.

         a   *b*   *c*   *d*

2.

       $\overline{AB}$

Describe the lines. Write *intersecting, perpendicular,* or *parallel.*

         a   *b*   *c*   *d*

3.

       __intersecting__

MIXED PRACTICE

Change each measurement to the larger unit.

         a   *b*   *c*

1. 48 in. = _____ ft   4,500 m = _____ km   20 qt = _____ gal

Change each measurement to the smaller unit.

         a   *b*   *c*

2. $3\frac{1}{2}$ T = _____ lb   3.5 L = _____ mL   98.4 yd = _____ ft

Angles

An **angle** is two rays with a common endpoint called a **vertex**.

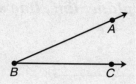

angle *ABC* or angle *CBA* or angle *B*

∠*ABC* or ∠*CBA* or ∠*B*

Angles are measured in **degrees** (°).

Angles are classified by their size.

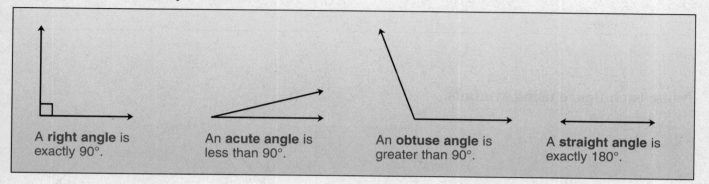

A **right angle** is exactly 90°.

An **acute angle** is less than 90°.

An **obtuse angle** is greater than 90°.

A **straight angle** is exactly 180°.

GUIDED PRACTICE

Name each angle using symbols.

1.

a

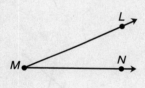

∠LMN

b

c

d

_____

_____

_____

Classify each angle. Write *right, acute, obtuse,* or *straight.*

a

2.

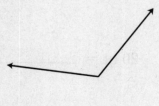

obtuse

b

c

d

_____

_____

_____

PRACTICE

Name each angle using symbols.

      a   *b*   *c*   *d*

1. 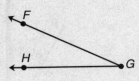   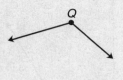   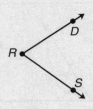

_____ _____ _____ _____

Classify each angle. Write *right, acute, obtuse,* or *straight*.

      a   *b*   *c*   *d*

2.   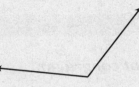   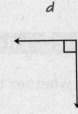

_____ _____ _____ _____

Use the drawing at right for Exercises 3–8.

3. Name an acute angle. _____

4. Name an angle with vertex *C*. _____

5. Name a right angle. _____

6. Name an obtuse angle. _____

7. Name an angle less than 90°. _____

8. Name a straight angle. _____

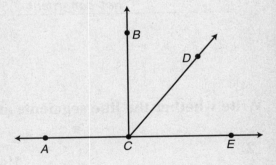

MIXED PRACTICE

Find each answer.

     a   *b*   *c*   *d*

1.
$$\begin{array}{r} 3.8 \\ \times 2.6 \\ \hline \end{array}$$

$$\begin{array}{r} \$5\,0 \\ -\ 1\,4.9\,9 \\ \hline \end{array}$$

$$\begin{array}{r} 3\,7.5 \\ +1\,8.7\,0\,6 \\ \hline \end{array}$$

$1\,4)\overline{1\,6\,2.4}$

Congruent Segments and Angles

Congruent line segments and angles have the same measure. The symbol for congruent is ≅.

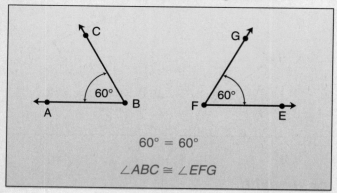

60° = 60°

∠ABC ≅ ∠EFG

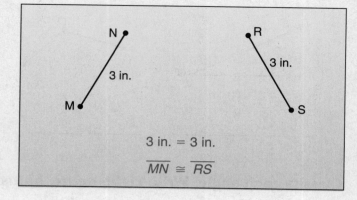

3 in. = 3 in.

$\overline{MN}$ ≅ $\overline{RS}$

GUIDED PRACTICE

Write whether the angles are *congruent* or *not congruent*.

a

b

1.

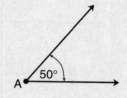

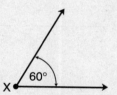

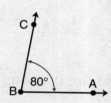

_____ not congruent _____   _____

Write whether the line segments are *congruent* or *not congruent*.

a

b

2.

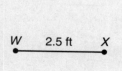

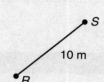

_____   _____

142

PRACTICE

Write whether the angles are *congruent* or *not congruent*.

           a   *b*

1.

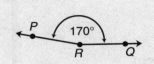 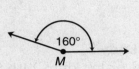 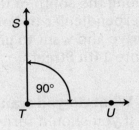 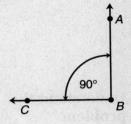

_____

Write whether the line segments are *congruent* or *not congruent*.

           a   *b*

2.

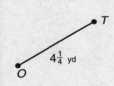 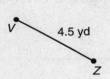 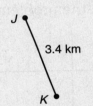 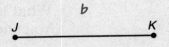

_____

Use a ruler to draw a line segment congruent to each given line segment.

           a   *b*

3.   A •————————————• B   J •————————————• K

MIXED PRACTICE

Find each answer.

    a   *b*   *c*   *d*

1. $\frac{1}{3} + \frac{7}{12} =$ $6\frac{1}{2} - \frac{4}{9} =$ $\frac{4}{5} \times \frac{2}{3} =$ $2\frac{5}{8} + \frac{1}{4} =$

Problem-Solving Strategy: Make a Drawing

Madison Drive and Jefferson Drive are parallel streets in Washington, D.C. Madison runs along the north side of the park and Jefferson runs along the south of the park. 14th Street intersects both streets and is perpendicular to both streets. If you are walking west on Jefferson Drive and want to get to Madison Drive, should you turn right or left onto 14th Street?

Understand the problem.

- **What do you want to know?**
  if you should turn right or left onto 14th Street

- **What information is given?**
  the description and directions of 3 streets in Washington, D.C.
  You are walking west on Jefferson Drive.

Plan how to solve it.

- **What strategy can you use?**
  You can make a drawing of the streets.

Solve it.

- **How can you use this strategy to solve the problem?**
  Draw and label the streets. Then follow the information in the problem to find Madison Drive from 14th Street.

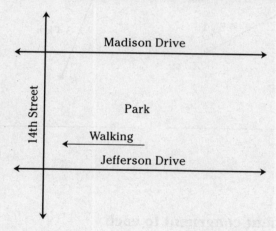

- **What is the answer?**
  You should turn right onto 14th Street.

Look back and check your answer.

- **Is your answer reasonable?**
  Reread the descriptions in the problem and check that they match your drawing.

  The answer matches the descriptions.
  It is reasonable.

Make a drawing to solve each problem.

1. Main Street runs east to west. Elm Street is perpendicular to and intersects Main Street. Taylor Avenue intersects both Main and Elm Streets at different points. What shape do the three streets form?

Answer _____

2. The town square has a statue at each corner. A bricked sidewalk starts at each statue and runs diagonally across the square. What kind of angles are formed by the intersection of the 4 sidewalks?

Answer _____

3. Andy and Maya hiked 1 mile north from their camp. Then they walked 3 miles east to the river. Next they went 5 miles south along the river, and from there, they walked 3 miles west. How far did they have to walk to get back to camp?

Answer _____

4. Peter and Marcia are building a stone wall that will be 38 feet long. Peter starts from one end and builds 9 feet of the wall. Marcia starts at the other end and builds 7 feet of the wall. How much of the wall is not built?

Answer _____

Perimeter of a Rectangle

Perimeter is the distance around a figure. To find the perimeter of a rectangle, count the number of units around the rectangle.

Find the perimeter of this rectangle by counting units.

Start at point *A*. Move clockwise and count the units from *A* to *B* (8), to *C* (13), to *D* (21), to *A* (26).

The perimeter of this rectangle is 26 units.

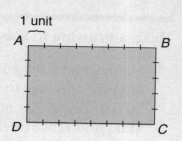

PRACTICE

Find the perimeter of each rectangle.

	a	*b*	*c*

1.

16 units

_____   _____   _____

2.

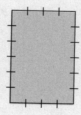

_____   _____   _____

3.

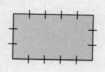

_____   _____   _____

4.

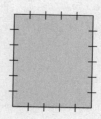

_____   _____   _____

Formula for Perimeter of a Rectangle

To find the perimeter of a rectangle, you can also use a **formula.**

Notice that the opposite sides of a rectangle are equal.

The formula, $P = 2l + 2w$, means the perimeter of a rectangle equals 2 times the length (l) plus 2 times the width (w).

Find the perimeter of this rectangle by using the formula.

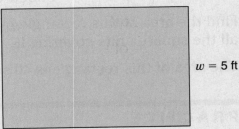

w = 5 ft

l = 8 ft

Write the formula.	$P = 2l + 2w$
Substitute the data.	$P = (2 \times 8) + (2 \times 5)$
Solve the problem.	$P = 16 + 10$
	$P = 26$

The perimeter of this rectangle is 26 feet.

PRACTICE

Find the perimeter of each rectangle by using the formula.

| a | b | c |

1. length = 15 in.
width = 12 in.
$P = 2l + 2w$
$P = (2 \times 15) + (2 \times 12)$
$P = 30 + 24$
$P = 54$ in.

length = 32 cm
width = 27 cm

width = 2 m
length = 2.5 m

2. width = 29 yd
length = 33 yd

length = 24 in.
width = 18 in.

length = $6\frac{1}{4}$ ft
width = $4\frac{1}{2}$ ft

3. length = 12.4 m
width = 10.5 m

width = 46 mm
length = 54 mm

length = 22 yd
width = 18 yd

4. length = 92 cm
width = 75 cm

width = 15.2 m
length = 18.6 m

length = 29 ft
width = 27 ft

Area of a Rectangle

Area is the number of **square units** needed to cover a figure.
To find the area of a rectangle, count the number of square
units covering the rectangle.

1 square unit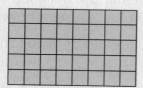

Find the area of this rectangle by counting
all the square units covering it.

The area of this rectangle is 40 square units.

PRACTICE

Find the area of each rectangle by counting the square units.

	a	b	c

1.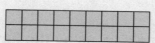

12 square units

2.

3.

4.

Formula for Area of a Rectangle

To find the area of a rectangle, you can also use a formula.

The formula, $A = lw$, means the area of a rectangle equals the length times the width.

Find the area of this rectangle by using the formula.

$w = 5$ ft

$l = 8$ ft

Write the formula. $A = l \times w$
Substitute the data. $A = 8 \times 5$
Solve the problem. $A = 40$

The area of this rectangle is 40 square feet.

Remember, write your answer in *square* units.

PRACTICE

Find the area of each rectangle by using the formula.

         a   *b*   *c*

1. length = 18 cm   length = 78 mm   length = $7\frac{1}{2}$ ft

    width = 15 cm   width = 42 mm   width = $1\frac{1}{2}$ ft

$A = l \times w$
$A = 18 \times 15$
$A = 270$ *square centimeters*

2. width = 3.8 m   length = 19 yd   width = 8 ft

    length = 6.5 m   width = 4 yd   length = 20 ft

3. length = 85 in.   width = 1.8 m   length = 17.5 cm

    width = 37 in.   length = 2.2 m   width = 4.3 cm

4. length = $4\frac{1}{2}$ yd   width = 9 m   length = 8 in.

    width = $2\frac{1}{4}$ yd   length = 13 m   width = $3\frac{1}{2}$ in.

Volume of a Rectangular Solid

Volume is the number of **cubic units** needed to fill a solid figure. To find the volume of a rectangular solid, count the number of cubic units in the rectangular box.

1 cubic unit

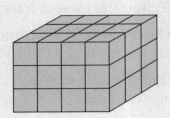

Find the volume of this rectangular solid by counting cubic units.

Count the number of cubes in the top layer.
Count the number of layers. Then multiply.

$$\begin{array}{r} 12 \\ \times\ 3 \\ \hline 36 \end{array}$$

The volume of this rectangular box is 36 cubic units.

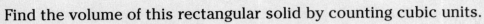

PRACTICE

Find the volume of each rectangular solid by counting the cubic units.

          a   *b*   *c*

1.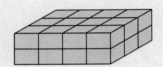

    24 cubic units

2.   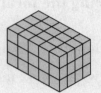   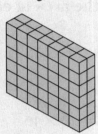

3. 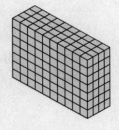   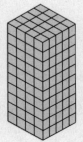   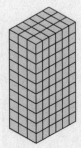

Formula for Volume of a Rectangular Solid

To find the volume of a rectangular solid, you can also use a formula.

The formula, $V = lwh$, means the volume of a rectangular solid equals the length times the width times the height.

Find the volume of this rectangular solid.

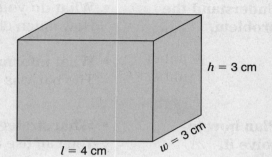

$h = 3$ cm
$l = 4$ cm
$w = 3$ cm

Write the formula. $V = l \times w \times h$
Substitute the data. $V = 4 \times 3 \times 3$
Solve the problem. $V = 36$

The volume of this rectangular solid is 36 cubic centimeters.

Remember, write your answer in *cubic* units.

PRACTICE

Find the volume of each rectangular solid. Use the formula.

	a	b	c

1.
a	b	c
length = 20 ft	length = 25 mm	length = 34 in.
width = 10 ft	width = 24 mm	width = 28 in.
height = 7 ft	height = 10 mm	height = 16 in.

$V = l \times w \times h$
$V = 20 \times 10 \times 7$
$V = 1,400$ cubic ft

2.
a	b	c
length = 4 cm	length = $12\frac{1}{2}$ in.	length = 15 ft
width = 1.5 cm	width = 5 in.	width = 12 ft
height = 2.6 cm	height = 20 in.	height = 8 ft

3.
a	b	c
length = 20 yd	length = 8 m	length = 12 yd
width = 16 yd	width = 5.5 m	width = $8\frac{1}{4}$ yd
height = 6 yd	height = 6.4 m	height = 10 yd

Problem-Solving Strategy: Use a Formula

The world's largest chocolate candy bar was made in England in 1998. It was 12.9 feet long, 4.9 feet wide, and 1 foot tall. How many cubic feet of chocolate were used to make the bar?

Understand the problem.

- **What do you want to know?**
  How much chocolate was in the candy bar?

- **What information is given?**
  The bar was 12.9 feet long, 4.9 feet wide, and 1 foot tall.

Plan how to solve it.

- **What strategy can you use?**
  You can use a formula.

Solve it.

- **How can you use this strategy to solve the problem?**
  Since a bar is a rectangular solid, you can use the formula for the volume of a rectangular solid.

  $$V = l \times w \times h$$

  $$V = 12.9 \times 4.9 \times 1$$

  $$V = 63.21$$

- **What is the answer?**
  The bar had 63.21 cubic feet of chocolate.

Look back and check your answer.

- **Is your answer reasonable?**
  You can estimate to check your answer.

  $$10 \times 5 \times 1 = 50$$

  The estimate is close to the answer.
  The answer is reasonable.

Use a formula to solve each problem.

1. The total capacity of your lungs is about the same as the volume of a 12 in. × 8 in. × 5 in. shoe box. About how many cubic inches of air can your lungs hold?

Answer _____

2. A regulation football field is 100 yards long and $53\frac{1}{3}$ yards wide. How many square yards of grass would you need to cover the whole field?

Answer _____

3. Greg's rectangular fish tank is 30.5 cm long, 18.6 cm wide, and 12 cm tall. How many cubic centimeters of water will fill Greg's fish tank?

Answer _____

4. A twin bed is 39 inches wide and 72 inches long. How long is a dust ruffle that goes around the bottom of a twin bed?

Answer _____

5. A professional soccer field is 75 meters wide and 110 meters long. Linda ran around the soccer field three times after practice. How far did she run?

Answer _____

6. Each can of paint covers 40 square feet. Each wall in Charlene's bedroom is 10 feet tall and 8 feet wide. How many cans does she need to paint the 4 walls?

Answer _____

153

Problem-Solving Applications

Solve.

1. The gymnasium floor measures 90 feet by 150 feet. What is the perimeter of the gymnasium floor?

   Answer _____

2. The window in a railroad car measures 24 inches by 21 inches. How many square inches of glass are in the window pane?

   Answer _____

3. The public swimming pool is 50 meters long, 20 meters wide, and 2 meters deep. How many cubic meters of water are needed to fill the pool?

   Answer _____

4. The playground is one-half as wide as it is long. It is 120 yards long. How much fencing is needed to enclose the entire playground?

   Answer _____

5. A cord of wood measures 128 cubic feet. How many cords are there in a stack of wood measuring 8 feet by 8 feet by 16 feet?

   Answer _____

6. Jake had a 24-inch by 30-inch painting framed at a cost of $0.49 an inch. How much did Jake pay for the framing?

   Answer _____

7. Find the cost, at $3.50 per square meter, of laying a concrete walk 100 meters long and 1.5 meters wide.

   Answer _____

8. The dimensions inside of a train car are 70 feet by $9\frac{1}{2}$ feet by 10 feet. What is the capacity of the car in cubic feet?

   Answer _____

Use the drawing at right for Exercises 1–7.

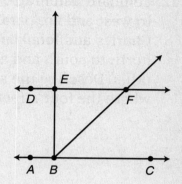

1. Name a point. _____

2. Name a line. _____

3. Name an acute angle. _____

4. Name a ray. _____

5. Name a pair of parallel lines. _____

6. Name a line segment. _____

7. Name two congruent angles. _____

Count the units to find the following.

       a   *b*   *c*

8. 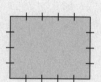   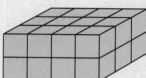

Perimeter _____   Area _____   Volume _____

Find the perimeter of each rectangle. Use the formula $P = 2l + 2w$.

a	*b*	*c*
9. length = 2.7 m	length = 90 cm	length = $11\frac{2}{3}$ yd
width = 1.4 m	width = 80 cm	width = $5\frac{2}{3}$ yd
_____	_____	_____

Find the area of each rectangle. Use the formula $A = l \times w$.

a	*b*	*c*
10. length = 21 mm	length = $42\frac{1}{2}$ in.	length = 3.9 cm
width = 8 mm	width = $30\frac{1}{2}$ in.	width = 1.7 cm
_____	_____	_____

Find the volume of each rectangle. Use the formula $V = l \times w \times h$.

a	*b*	*c*
11. length = 8 yd	length = 10 m	length = 25 ft
width = 6 yd	width = 3.4 m	width = $2\frac{1}{4}$ ft
height = 9 yd	height = 5 m	height = 4 ft
_____	_____	_____

Make a drawing to solve each problem.

12. Lombard and Pratt Streets both run east to west and are parallel to each other. Charles and Franklin Streets both run north to south and are parallel to each other. Describe the shape that is formed where the four streets meet.

13. Karen, Tremont, Joe, and Anita sat on the same side of the picnic table. Karen sat between Joe and Tremont. Joe sat between Anita and Karen. Which two people sat at the ends of the table?

Answer _____

Answer _____

Use a formula to solve each problem.

14. In 1506, Leonardo da Vinci painted the *Mona Lisa* on a piece of pinewood, 30 in. by $20\frac{7}{8}$ in. How much wood was needed to frame the *Mona Lisa?*

15. A compact disc case is 14 cm long, 12.5 cm wide, and 1 cm tall. What is the area of the case's top cover? What is the volume of the case?

Answer _____

Answer _____

Write the place name for the 6 in each number.

a b

1. 643,517 _____   167,025,908 _____

Compare. Write <, >, or =.

     a b c

2. 364 _____ 355   89,435 _____ 98,452   5,423 _____ 5,423

Add or subtract.

a	b	c	d
3. 1,0 9 4	2,3 4 2	1,2 4 4	9,3 4 6
+ 3 0 5	+5,0 7 7	− 9 5 5	−6,8 3 6

a	b	c	d
4. 1 3,1 3 3			
4,7 8 5	2 4 8,9 1 0	7 1 2,1 3 8	4 3 6,0 0 0
+1 0,6 0 1	−1 5 1,4 8 7	+2 7 5,9 3 7	−1 8 2,3 9 7

Multiply or divide.

a	b	c	d
5. 3 8	4)2,7 2 4	7 1	8)1 6,3 4 9
× 3		×5 2	

a	b	c	d
6. 2 3)4,8 6 3	9 1,8 1 5	4 0 5	5 1 9
	× 4 4	×2 6 9	×1 8 0

Estimate.

a	b	c	d
7. 6 2 →	7 8 →	6 3 7 →	7)3 6 1 →
+2 8 →	×3 2 →	−4 1 2 →	

a	b	c	d
8. 7 8 9 →	2 7)6 1 8 →	5 1 7 →	5 3 →
− 4 5 →		× 8 1 →	−1 8 →

Final Review

Add. Simplify.

	a	*b*	*c*	*d*	*e*

9.

$\begin{array}{r} \frac{5}{8} \\ + \frac{1}{2} \\ \hline \end{array}$ $\begin{array}{r} 2\frac{6}{7} \\ +4 \\ \hline \end{array}$ $\begin{array}{r} \frac{4}{6} \\ +\frac{2}{5} \\ \hline \end{array}$ $\begin{array}{r} \frac{2}{3} \\ +1\frac{3}{8} \\ \hline \end{array}$ $\begin{array}{r} 11\frac{7}{12} \\ +5\frac{3}{4} \\ \hline \end{array}$

10.

$\begin{array}{r} 11 \\ +6\frac{11}{14} \\ \hline \end{array}$ $\begin{array}{r} \frac{3}{4} \\ +\frac{2}{6} \\ \hline \end{array}$ $\begin{array}{r} 7\frac{3}{10} \\ +\frac{2}{5} \\ \hline \end{array}$ $\begin{array}{r} 4\frac{7}{12} \\ +5\frac{5}{12} \\ \hline \end{array}$ $\begin{array}{r} 2\frac{4}{9} \\ +3\frac{1}{2} \\ \hline \end{array}$

Subtract. Simplify.

	a	*b*	*c*	*d*	*e*

11.

$\begin{array}{r} \frac{2}{3} \\ -\frac{3}{5} \\ \hline \end{array}$ $\begin{array}{r} 6 \\ -\frac{3}{8} \\ \hline \end{array}$ $\begin{array}{r} 26 \\ -18\frac{5}{6} \\ \hline \end{array}$ $\begin{array}{r} 9\frac{1}{3} \\ -5\frac{1}{4} \\ \hline \end{array}$ $\begin{array}{r} 15\frac{1}{6} \\ -4\frac{5}{6} \\ \hline \end{array}$

12.

$\begin{array}{r} 17\frac{5}{7} \\ -11\frac{1}{3} \\ \hline \end{array}$ $\begin{array}{r} 34\frac{1}{10} \\ -\frac{2}{5} \\ \hline \end{array}$ $\begin{array}{r} 34\frac{1}{10} \\ -4\frac{7}{8} \\ \hline \end{array}$ $\begin{array}{r} 40\frac{2}{5} \\ -39\frac{5}{6} \\ \hline \end{array}$ $\begin{array}{r} 7\frac{2}{9} \\ -4\frac{5}{6} \\ \hline \end{array}$

Multiply. Simplify.

	a	*b*	*c*

13. $\frac{4}{5} \times \frac{10}{12} =$ $\qquad$ $\frac{5}{6} \times 7 =$ $\qquad$ $6 \times 2\frac{1}{4} =$

14. $8\frac{1}{3} \times \frac{3}{5} =$ $\qquad$ $4\frac{3}{8} \times 3\frac{1}{5} =$ $\qquad$ $7\frac{3}{7} \times 1\frac{1}{2} =$

Divide. Simplify.

	a	*b*	*c*

15. $\frac{8}{9} \div \frac{1}{3} =$ $\qquad$ $12 \div \frac{2}{5} =$ $\qquad$ $\frac{3}{4} \div 5\frac{1}{2} =$

16. $5\frac{6}{7} \div \frac{4}{7} =$ $\qquad$ $2\frac{2}{3} \div 1\frac{1}{6} =$ $\qquad$ $3\frac{3}{4} \div 1\frac{1}{9} =$

Final Review

Write as a decimal.

a   *b*

17. five and two hundredths _____   thirty-two thousandths _____

Write each fraction as a decimal.

a	*b*	*c*
18. $\frac{3}{10}$ _____	$\frac{112}{100}$ _____	$\frac{3}{4}$ _____

Add or subtract. Write zeros as needed.

a	*b*	*c*	*d*
19. $\begin{array}{r} 1\,8.2 \\ +\ \ 6.9 \\ \hline \end{array}$	$\begin{array}{r} \$\ 5.6\,2 \\ +\ \ 7.8\,4 \\ \hline \end{array}$	$\begin{array}{r} 6.2\,7\,3 \\ +1\,3.8\,4 \\ \hline \end{array}$	$\begin{array}{r} 2\,8.9 \\ +5\,7.6\,1\,3 \\ \hline \end{array}$
20. $\begin{array}{r} 2\,8.1\,2 \\ -\ \ 6.0\,4 \\ \hline \end{array}$	$\begin{array}{r} \$\ 3\,2.9\,0 \\ -\ 1\,5.4\,6 \\ \hline \end{array}$	$\begin{array}{r} 3 \\ -2.9\,3 \\ \hline \end{array}$	$\begin{array}{r} 5.2 \\ -0.0\,2\,7 \\ \hline \end{array}$

Estimate each sum or difference by rounding to the nearest one.

a	*b*	*c*	*d*
21. $\begin{array}{r} 6.9 \rightarrow \\ +5.4 \rightarrow \\ \hline \end{array}$	$\begin{array}{r} 1\,8.7\,6 \rightarrow \\ +\ \ 9.2\ \ \rightarrow \\ \hline \end{array}$	$\begin{array}{r} 9.1 \rightarrow \\ -3.3 \rightarrow \\ \hline \end{array}$	$\begin{array}{r} 8\,3.7 \rightarrow \\ -2\,4.5 \rightarrow \\ \hline \end{array}$

Multiply or divide. Write zeros as needed.

a	*b*	*c*
22. $0.913 \times 10 =$ _____	$25.9 \times 100 =$ _____	$4.17 \times 1{,}000 =$ _____
23. $51.4 \div 10 =$ _____	$272.6 \div 100 =$ _____	$185 \div 1{,}000 =$ _____

a	*b*	*c*	*d*
24. $\begin{array}{r} 5\,2.7 \\ \times\ \ 1.4 \\ \hline \end{array}$	$\begin{array}{r} 2\,1.8 \\ \times\ \ 0.9 \\ \hline \end{array}$	$\begin{array}{r} 0.3\,6 \\ \times 0.8\,5 \\ \hline \end{array}$	$\begin{array}{r} 8.4\,1 \\ \times\ \ 1\,0.7 \\ \hline \end{array}$

25. $6\overline{)3\,7.2}$ $0.5\overline{)1\,8\,4.5}$ $0.8\,3\overline{)7.0\,5\,5}$ $7\,8\overline{)1\,1.7}$

Divide. Round to the place named.

a	*b*	*c*
nearest tenth	nearest cent	nearest hundredths
26. $4\,1\overline{)7.3\,8}$	$1\,3\overline{)\$\,7\,1.6\,4}$	$0.8\overline{)5.5\,4}$

Final Review

Change each measurement to the smaller unit.

	a	*b*	*c*
27.	$2\frac{1}{2}$ ft = _____ in.	$3\frac{1}{4}$ lb = _____ oz	5 qt = _____ c
28.	00.6 kg = _____ g	17.8 L = _____ mL	9.4 m = _____ cm

Change each measurement to the larger unit.

	a	*b*	*c*
29.	5,000 lb = _____ T	8 ft = _____ yd	36 qt = _____ gal
30.	71 mm = _____ cm	13.5 g = _____ kg	900 mL = _____ L

Find each answer.

	a	*b*	*c*
31.	6 ft 4 in. + 18 ft 7 in.	8 kg 64 g − 5 kg 200 g	12 lb 8 oz + 15 lb 9 oz
32.	42 gal 8 pt × 3	5 km 500 m − 3 km 800 m	4)9 L 600 mL

Use the drawing at right for Exercises 33–38.

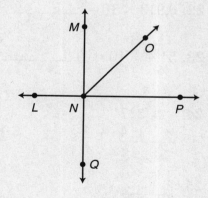

33. Name a ray. _____

34. Name a line segment. _____

35. Name an obtuse angle. _____

36. Name 2 congruent angles. _____

37. Name 2 perpendicular lines. _____

38. Name a line. _____

Use the formulas to find the following.

$$P = 2l + 2w \qquad A = l \times w \qquad V = l \times w \times h$$

	a	*b*	*c*
39.	length = 5.8 cm width = 12.8 cm	length = $8\frac{3}{4}$ in. width = $4\frac{1}{3}$ in.	length = 6.5 ft width = 3.4 ft height = 2 ft
	Perimeter _____	Area _____	Volume _____